Praise for *Be Feel Think Do*

"Be Feel Think Do *artfully combines personal narrative and poignant insights as Anne guides her reader to the sustainable source of happiness that is our natural state.*"

— Deepak Chopra, M.D., #1 *New York Times* best-selling author

"*A beautiful book about what happens when your soul wakes you up to who you really are, when you follow your heart, and learn to trust the wild inner knowing to discover a life beyond what you thought possible. In the midst of so many self-help spiritual books, Anne Bérubé has penned a memoir well worth reading.*"

— Colette Baron-Reid, best-selling inspirational author of *The Map* and *Uncharted*

"*With her moving memoir, Anne Bérubé invites us to find ourselves inside her story of awakening to the soul's journey. She gracefully unpacks her experiences so they may become a mirror for us to identify our own pathway. Anne's heartfelt offering is a genuine invitation to reunite with what matters most.*"

— Nancy Levin, author of *Worthy*

"*Anne's soul-searching story is gripping and powerfully written. Witnessing her transformation redefines possibility. If you love memoirs that read like a good romantic novel, then she does not disappoint. If you enjoy lessons interwoven into great storytelling, then you will love* Be Feel Think Do. *You will see clearly your own fork in the road and how the brave path pays off with the real goods in life.*"

— Julie Daniluk, author of *The Hot Detox Plan*

BE
· · ·
FEEL
· · ·
THINK
· · ·
DO

ANNE BÉRUBÉ, Ph.D.

BE
FEEL
THINK
DO

A Memoir

HAY HOUSE, INC.

Carlsbad, California • New York City
London • Sydney • Johannesburg
Vancouver • New Delhi

Published and distributed in the United States by: Hay House, Inc.: www.hayhouse.com® • *Published and distributed in Australia by:* Hay House Australia Pty. Ltd.: www.hayhouse.com.au • *Published and distributed in the United Kingdom by:* Hay House UK, Ltd.: www.hayhouse.co.uk • *Published and distributed in the Republic of South Africa by:* Hay House SA (Pty), Ltd.: www.hayhouse.co.za • *Distributed in Canada by:* Raincoast Books: www.raincoast.com • *Published in India by:* Hay House Publishers India: www.hayhouse.co.in

Cover design: Tricia Breidenthal • *Interior design:* Riann Bender

Cataloging-in-Publication Data on file with the Library of Congress

Tradepaper ISBN: 978-1-4019-5115-3

10 9 8 7 6 5 4 3 2 1
1st edition, May 2017

In memory of Wayne Dyer
"Good things are going to happen."

———— • ————

To Olivier, my moon, and Hanalei, my sun.
To Paul, my soulmate.
To my father, my cheerleader, and
to my mother, my greatest teacher.

———— • ————

CONTENTS

Foreword   xi

Introduction   xv

PART I: Do Think Feel Be: Remembering the Soul   1

Chapter 1:   Time Slowed Way Down   3
Chapter 2:   Making a Move   5
Chapter 3:   The One, Maybe   9
Chapter 4:   Course Correction   17
Chapter 5:   Granny   21
Chapter 6:   A Wild Inner Knowing   25
Chapter 7:   Displacement   29
Chapter 8:   Summer Reading   31
Chapter 9:   Beyond the Break   35
Chapter 10: Two Years, Two Continents, Two Degrees,
                 and a Baby   39
Chapter 11: Where's the Exit?   45
Chapter 12: Finding Mother   49
Chapter 13: Wine-and-Cheese Thesis   57
Chapter 14: A Shamanic Journey   63
Chapter 15: An Autopoetic Life   71
Chapter 16: Heart-Shaped Compass   77
Chapter 17: The End of the World   83
Chapter 18: The Space between Two People in a Hug   85
Chapter 19: A Gift   89

PART II: Be Feel Think Do: Living the Soul   95

Chapter 20:   Four Simple Words   99
Chapter 21:   An Inside Job   103
Chapter 22:   We Are Eternal   109
Chapter 23:   The Externally Referenced Life   113
Chapter 24:   Gift of the Morning   117
Chapter 25:   Seated Within   121
Chapter 26:   Gateway to the Soul   127
Chapter 27:   Creative Body   133
Chapter 28:   Language of the Soul   137
Chapter 29:   The Art of Breathing   143
Chapter 30:   The Tree Bends toward the Light   151
Chapter 31:   Heart the New Brain   155
Chapter 32:   First Choice, Last Freedom   161
Chapter 33:   Mirrors and Metaphors   171
Chapter 34:   Conscious Creator   181
Chapter 35:   Authentic Communication   185
Chapter 36:   Same Source, Different Points of Entry   193
Chapter 37:   Self-Love as an Act of Service   199
Chapter 38:   Living Fearlessly   207

Afterword   213
Endnotes   225
Acknowledgments   227
About the Author   229

FOREWORD

————— • —————

I have been deeply touched by the contents of this book that you are holding in your hands, and even more so by my personal friendship with Anne Bérubé.

Anne came into my life through a series of synchronicities, because of our relationship with the late, great Dr. Wayne Dyer.

Some of you may be familiar with my story of dealing with an advanced cancer, which took me to death's door and beyond. Thankfully, I survived and lived to tell the tale of my sojourn in the other realm. Wayne Dyer discovered my story and introduced me to his vast audience. As I traveled the world, sharing the stage with him, I was blessed to meet Anne and her husband, Paul, whom Wayne considered close friends—almost family, in fact.

Both Anne and Paul were often in the audience during these events, and over time, our friendship grew. But the bond was sealed by a tragic event—the death of our dear mutual friend, Wayne. Both Anne and I were impacted in our own way, and were both still sensing his presence and his guidance.

One day, shortly after Wayne's passing, Anne and Paul coordinated a speaking tour of Canada for me. This was something they used to do for Wayne. Usually, when I go on tour, an assistant accompanies me. This is someone who familiarizes themselves with all the details of my schedule and appointments for the duration of the trip, so as to keep me on track while I focus on my presentation material. On this particular occasion, my assigned speaking assistant was called away for an emergency (but not life-threatening) surgery and could not accompany me, and it was too short notice to find someone else to replace her—particularly someone who could familiarize themselves with all the logistics the trip would entail. Stressed at the thought of trying to familiarize myself with all the details of the upcoming tour without assistance (an area that I'm not particularly good at keeping track of), I was feeling a little lost and worried about how I'd cope.

However, just days before departing home, I received a phone call from Anne. Somehow sensing my feeling of uncertainty and despair, Anne said, "I'll accompany you! I can keep track of all your flights, and your hotels, and everything else in your itinerary. I've done it for Deepak Chopra; I've done it for Wayne. Don't worry. I'll accompany you from start to finish of your Canadian tour!" The relief I felt was palpable when I put down the phone, and a weight was lifted off my shoulders!

So from there, we embarked on a two-week tour of Canada, which started from Anne's hometown of Halifax. From the time she greeted me at the airport in Halifax, there was an instant connection, and we found ourselves talking about everything, from our dreams to our deepest hopes and wishes to where our lives were now. We also talked about our dear friend Wayne and how he had left so suddenly. During our conversation, one thing became clear. We felt that somehow, from beyond the veil, Wayne had orchestrated for this to happen. He had orchestrated for us to have this time together, to get to know each other and seal our friendship.

It was during this trip that Anne told me she was writing this book you are now reading. Wayne had encouraged her to put her journey onto paper, much like he had encouraged me to do the same. As we spoke, we both felt a sense of sadness that he was no longer here in the physical world to see her completed work, but we felt confident that he was still there, watching over us from the other side of the veil. He was probably feeling joy, smiling at the thought of Anne taking his advice to heart and authoring a book about her life!

In the first part of this beautiful book, you will get to know Anne as she shares the story of her life with uncommon candor. What I love about Anne is that she doesn't hold back on sharing her true self with vulnerability. In these pages, you will get to know a woman who is both brave and sensitive, and you will also get to know her beautiful family.

In the second part of the book, she shares all the wisdom she learned from the challenges in her life and gives practical tips on how to apply it. She breaks them down to make them easy to understand and accessible.

If Wayne were alive, I'm certain he would have been the one to write the foreword to this beautiful book. I am honored to do this on his behalf and play a small role in helping to bring this story into the world. Please enjoy it, and enjoy getting to know Anne through her words, as much as I did.

With love,
Anita Moorjani

INTRODUCTION

—— • ——

The seed for this book was planted in the spring of 2001, and like all good love stories, it starts with the feeling of being hit by a half-ton truck. Although in this case, I am being literal.

By 2008, I was well on my way to becoming a university professor with a Ph.D. in French literature. I spent my time with my nose buried in books applying academic literary theory to contemporary texts. As I prepared for my thesis defense, I realized that somehow along the way I had become far more interested in the characters and the authors than I was in the literary theories I was supposed to be applying. I deeply longed to understand their humanity and the forces that propelled them to make the choices they were making as they created their narratives. I cared most about what brought them meaning and joy.

It had been my dream to become a professor of literature. But I had fallen madly in love with the creative human heart. I became captivated with the soul and its secrets and I couldn't go back. I wanted to understand everything I could about human beings: what inspires us to create; why we care so deeply; how we navigate changes and difficult times; and, most importantly, what brings us an inner sense of peace, fulfillment, and happiness. My academic interests took a backseat to this pursuit, and these fascinations would become the driving force behind this book.

Anyone who has worked through personal transformation and deep exploration knows that it can be a messy process. Years of struggle, "ah-ha" moments, pain, healings, radical transformation, and heartbreak yielded to deep understanding. As I sifted through the layers and layers of tightly held conditioned beliefs about life, myself, and other people, I slowly began to surrender to a process of unbecoming and becoming. I noticed a progression emerge—a way of living that made sense and supported a deeply spiritual life, one I had been craving for as long as I could remember.

This progression allowed for a spirituality that was not simply intellectual nor solely esoteric, but embodied through and through and integrated in my entire being as well as in all aspects of my life: family, relationships, career, passions. This way of living was incredibly clear and compassionate, grounded and enlightened. It required a lot more *feeling* than ever before and a whole lot of inner stillness, which I refer to as *being*.

Like most people, I was used to living solely in and from my head, reacting out of habit, navigating on autopilot, never stopping to really ask the question *why?* Why did I do the things I did and make the choices I made? Most of my energy and attention was focused on thinking about what I should do next based on what had happened in the past. Feelings and matters of the soul barely had a place. I was following this progression: *do think feel be.*

Along the way, as new information was presented to me and as I dove deep into the inner field of my body, I began to allow more *be* and more *feel* to show up in my life and eventually made them a daily priority. Naturally, this progression emerged: *be feel think do*. This simple shift in the order in which I engaged life changed everything.

This is how I came to discover *be feel think do* and why I want to share my journey and insights with you. It brought a whole new, expanded, and mystical dimension to my life, one I could never have foreseen, and I know it can for you as well.

Just like a plant bends toward the light and needs it to live, our attention as we bend toward *be*—toward our soul—nourishes and enlivens our daily existence. This is my story. I hope it resonates with you and helps you remember who you truly are.

SOUL
(noun)
/sōl/

———— • ————

1. *the immaterial essence, animating principle, or
actuating cause of an individual life*
2. *the spiritual principle embodied in human beings, all
rational and spiritual beings, or the universe*
3. *a person's total self*
4. *the moral or emotional nature of human beings*
5. *the ability of a person to feel kindness and sympathy
for others, to appreciate beauty and art, etc.*[1]

———— • ————

PART I

DO

THINK

FEEL

BE

REMEMBERING

THE

SOUL

CHAPTER 1

TIME SLOWED WAY DOWN

———— • ————

L oud, ear shattering, life altering. And then dark. Just dark. Minutes, maybe seconds go by, it's hard to tell. When I open my eyes, I realize my lungs aren't working and I panic. Then it is dark again, and when I open my eyes this time, I see Mike's face through the passenger window that has shattered all over my body. His eyes portray shock and he is frantically trying to pull me out of the car through the passenger window as strangers behind him try to pull him away from me, telling him not to move me. He has a death grip on my arm.

And then it goes dark again.

It's surreal and difficult to explain the experience of the entire body shaken in such a violent manner. Time stops, or at least it slows way, way down.

It takes several minutes for my awareness to catch up to what was happening.

In the darkness of unconsciousness is when I see it. My life. My choice. It rolls out in front of my mind's eye like a movie.

Clear as day. I know it is my life I am witnessing. But it is not the one I am presently living. I see myself loving deeply and lots of people loving me deeply. I see myself writing and teaching. I am exuberant. I have childlike awe. I am joyful and peaceful. I am bold and I am clear. I see myself surfing with Paul, having children with Paul. I see a life filled with adventure and meaning. I see what love without conditions looks like.

But more importantly, I *feel* all those things. I experience inside my being what it feels like to live that life. I am connected with everything and everyone around me. I am this reality. In the presence of this vision, I experience an overwhelming feeling of love rushing through my body. It is the most amazing thing I have ever felt. In the vision, I remember the intimacy of feelings I'd experienced the summer before and *know* that the experience is coming back for me, coming to bring me back home.

CHAPTER 2

MAKING A MOVE

———— • ————

E verything began to change when I met Paul.

But before I tell you about Paul, let me set the scene. It was the spring of 2000. I was 22 and living in Halifax, Nova Scotia, with a long-term boyfriend. Mike and I met during my third and last year of my Photography degree at a college in Montreal when I was 19. I had just spent three fun-filled and wild years of living on my own in the big city, and I was now graduating and felt the pressure of not knowing my next step. I was more lost than ever before. I had left my hometown to escape my high school identity and reinvent myself. But three years later, I was still searching.

When Mike and I first spoke, I was a mess. I was smoking a cigarette and drinking a coffee outside the campus, wearing baggy shorts and a baggy shirt that belonged to my boyfriend, a bass player in a punk band, and my hair was crimped chaos thanks to the tightly braided pigtails I had sported at a concert the night before. For reasons unknown, he approached me and struck up a conversation. Mike was wearing a crisp shirt and a leather-sleeved jacket sporting our school crest. He was a first-year architecture student and seemed to have things figured out. We were so completely different, but his personality was attractive to me. He was incredibly smart, assured, and had known for a long time who he was and where he was headed in life. Floundering, I saw him as a safe haven, an anchor. He made me feel safe at a time when I felt quite confused and disillusioned with my life. After years of trying on different identities, the role of serious student and committed girlfriend had the allure of being refreshingly stable. Obviously, a new wardrobe was required.

Although we were French, he suggested we attend an out-of-province university in English Canada, and it felt like a smart plan. Growing up in rural Quebec, I don't remember even hearing the word *university* until late in my teen years. Even still, it was a foreign concept. No one in my family had gone on to do an undergraduate degree, let alone a graduate degree. So when Mike sold me on the idea, sharing stories of his prestigious older brother, an accomplished professor in England, I felt a whole new world was opening up for me. I held on to this buoy as tightly as I could, even though I was already having second thoughts about our relationship.

It was difficult for me to find myself within the relationship because my lack of self-awareness and self-assurance were no match for the strength of Mike's convictions and his decisiveness about our future. He always made more sense than I ever could. I concluded I was being unreasonable, because if one were to write a wish list, this man would check all the boxes. And besides that, I told myself that I should be strong enough to find myself regardless of his opinions. So we packed our bags, doubled down on our commitment by adopting a puppy, and moved east to a small university town of 5,000 in rural Nova Scotia.

From the outside looking in, it looked like we had it all figured out. A nice apartment, a car, a dog. We were both enrolled in professional programs at university and were on the fast track to financially secure careers. We had a plan and we were sticking to it. To all appearances, we were a happy couple. But judging by my day-to-day thoughts and feelings, I was not happy.

To be fair, I didn't really know what happiness meant, how it looked, or what it felt like at that time. I was driven to obtain all of the things I had been told would make me happy: a sensible education, friends, a stable career, and a boyfriend I would one day marry.

Mike and I disagreed on many things. In the heat of arguments, I couldn't find my grounding or my own voice. I didn't have the self-confidence needed to speak my truth. In the rare instances when I did take a stand, it would be to attempt to win an argument so I could feel at least a little validated. I was searching for a different way of living, and because I didn't know what it was yet, I couldn't fight for it, advocate for it, or advocate for me. I didn't have the language yet. More accurately, I had forgotten the language. I felt trapped during these arguments. Mike's intellect was so sharp that most of the time I would retreat, defeated, deflated. I couldn't gain perspective. Seeking happiness in his approval made me miserable.

I didn't know yet that happiness was an inside job and ultimately had nothing to do with him, even though I had had a glimpse of it back in Montreal. A few years back, on my mother's recommendation, I had taken a one-day course called Who Am I? During that day I felt something awaken inside me. When I came home to share my experience with Mike, he quickly convinced me that it was all pseudo-psychology and was feeding a fantasy. It wasn't real and I would be disappointed sooner or later. Somehow, I believed what he said and put that experience in the back of my mind. My sense of self was so fragmented I couldn't make up my own mind about what was true for *me*, much less trust it.

CHAPTER 3

THE ONE, MAYBE

———— • ————

A few months later, Mike and I were still living together in Halifax, and a new person quietly inserted himself into my life.

Paul was a brunch regular at the Libertine Café, where I worked as a waiter downtown. Unbeknownst to me, Paul and his friends had been coming to the restaurant every Sunday for an entire year, always asking to be seated in my section. I was incredibly self-conscious of my thick French accent and broken English, but apparently this had been good for business. Years later, I would discover that many of the English boys in my section found my accent charming.

One night, Paul surprised me by asking if I would like to come work for him. He was opening a fine-dining restaurant and told me what an honor it would be to employ his favorite waitress in the city. I didn't know I was his favorite waitress! I actually didn't really know this man at all, except as a customer. Nevertheless, something propelled me to drive an hour down Nova Scotia's South Shore the next weekend to check out this new restaurant.

Being in the presence of Paul that afternoon, surrounded by the ocean and the rugged land of Nova Scotia's South Shore, I felt transported. For a few hours, it was as if I had been plucked out of my current life and placed into an alternate reality—one that felt familiar and true to something deep inside me. I surprised myself when I said yes to Paul that very day, I didn't even take time to think about it.

When I arrived home later, all of this was very hard to explain to Mike. He didn't understand how I could make such a rash decision to leave a good-paying job in the city for a restaurant in the country that was just starting out. I couldn't explain my decision logically, nor did I wish to explain the mysterious pull to Paul and this place. Something had been awakened in me. This time, I had to answer the call.

Enter Shirley MacLaine. I'm not kidding. Two weeks after accepting the job, I was in a bookstore, and her book literally fell off the shelf at my feet. It was *The Camino*, and when I cracked it open, here's what I read: "It is mankind's moral obligation to seek joy through the feeling of Divinity within his or her own being." I read it over and over again. To say it grabbed my attention would be a massive understatement. A quick look at my life clearly showed that this kind of joy and "Divinity" had not been guiding my decisions so far. I had been led by a logical understanding of what I should want and what I should accomplish based on other people's expectation of me, real or made up. MacLaine's words spoke directly to my chest, like a spark, with the potential to burst into flames.

I realize now MacLaine was referring to a joy that lives in each of us, and has nothing to do with what we do, what we have, how we are perceived, or what we accomplish in life, but is our very essence and who we are. This spark exists in all of us and awaits to be reawakened.

Although I could feel the truth of the idea in my chest, this feeling of deep resonance was immediately countered by a sensible voice in my head that said, *Just a little too good to be true, don't you think?*

When I came home that evening and shared with Mike what I had experienced, our conversation reinforced my doubts in MacLaine's message. It seemed to make Mike upset, agitated, and even fearful, as if pondering such abstract ideas would deter us from our well-thought-out life plan and drive me away from him. He didn't want to talk about it at all, so I left it alone.

That summer, Paul and I became close friends. I had found a kindred spirit, someone I could discuss life's big questions with, the ones I had been pondering. We both shared an insatiable desire to understand the deeper dimensions of life and to support each other on the journey. In his presence, it felt like everything and anything was possible. He wasn't afraid to be vulnerable and sensitive, and he had such courage to leap and take chances in business, in play, and in friendships. This sense of limitlessness was new to me, and he would include me in this beautiful, expansive exploration with such confidence in my capabilities. His mere presence granted an unspoken permission to dare. It was the first time I had experienced unconditional love, a genuine reflection of deep acceptance and endless possibilities, with no opposite. I felt fully and completely seen and supported no matter what surfaced. Feeling deeply loved and simultaneously free was a brand-new experience for me.

Paul was a wonderful chef and was passionate about food. On nights when we'd have to work late, once all the customers had left, he'd prepare the most delicious meal for us and we'd talk for hours in the candlelit restaurant. During the hot summer days we'd take breaks in between shifts and frolic in the gullied rock formations on the shore, sliding down seaweed-covered boulders in the crashing surf. I loved glancing at Paul's strong and defined back when he wore his swim trunks, heading out to surf or looking for fish to spear. As the summer went on, everything about him pulled me into his playful and magical world. I wished I had met him earlier in my life, when we were children, so we could have played together. It was like I had missed him even though I didn't know him until now. He was on my mind constantly, even when I wasn't at work. I was falling in love but didn't have any frame of reference for a love that looked and felt like this. So I placed it in the category of mind-blowing friendship and continued to try and make my current relationship work.

My worldview was challenged again when Paul and I went to visit a psychic his mother had recommended. I hadn't seen a psychic before, although it intrigued me since I'd read about spiritual communication in *The Camino*. We drove to an old country house by the ocean surrounded by windswept English-style gardens. An eccentric-looking woman with beautiful deep blue eyes welcomed us. We were having separate readings, so she asked me to come in first. I sat on her couch in the middle of her sunroom. She closed her eyes and mumbled a few words, and when she opened her eyes, she was staring at me intensely. She began to speak to me in a very different voice than before, like she was another person.

She told me I was very creative, intuitive, and that one day, I could do what she does. She said I had a lot of protection around me, lots of spiritual guidance. All of this was so new to me. I listened, but I wasn't sure what to make of it. She also said Paul and I had shared many lifetimes and had supported each other through various life lessons. I had never heard about past lives, but I loved thinking about my existence through that lens. It felt wide and spacious. She also talked about Mike, saying I was done learning what I was here to learn with him. She said my desire to help him heal and understand the world differently would not be fulfilled as he was here for a different purpose. I knew inside my heart she was right. I could feel that truth. Then she said, "Your relationship with Paul is the best relationship for you in this lifetime. But you still get to choose." I knew inside of me *exactly* what she was saying and felt the resonance of this truth throughout my whole body. The flame within me was validated, and this knowledge brought such liberating freedom. In that moment I saw how my beliefs about what a relationship should be were based on my insecurities and what I had been conditioned to believe it should look like. The only part I had difficulty with was the choice part. I didn't want to have choices. The choice gave me a responsibility, and I didn't like that.

Then the psychic told Paul I was his soul mate and that he would not fall in love with anyone else in this lifetime. No pressure! But this validated Paul's feelings of who I was to him. Paul knew how to listen to his heart. He had known his strong feelings for me for a while.

It didn't take long for me to end my relationship with Mike. Paul and I spent the rest of the summer together as a couple and even moved in together in the fall. Our relationship was bigger than life, like we were being guided from one expanding experience to another by a force that existed behind the curtain but had such an intelligence. We had clear foresight of what was possible together. It was bliss with no opposite.

The relationship evolved so fast that the ground moved underneath me, and my world was shaken. I was so overwhelmed with the intensity of such a foreign feeling that I couldn't make sense of it. I didn't fully believe this kind of love was real. How was it that he saw all these wonderful things about me when I couldn't?

I began to test the boundaries and strength of his love. If it was this perfect, powerful thing, then surely it could withstand anything I threw at it. I needed it to be worth the imagined future I had given up. Although, ironically, I would never have thought to test Mike's love this way.

Perhaps Paul's love was too much for me to handle, or perhaps it was too big of a responsibility for me to live up to a love I didn't understand. I was scared that as he got to really know me and discover the ugly bits inside, he would wake up one morning and realize he had fallen for a girl who didn't actually exist. He would see who I really was and leave. If I was going to lose a love like that, it would be on my own terms—so I started to hit him with the really ugly bits.

How much love could I hold back before he stopped loving me? How late would I have to stay out to make him jealous? Could we take a break? How long? There was a lot of drama and a lot of hurt. But he never left and he never stopped loving me.

Less than four months after Paul and I moved in together, during a particularly difficult period, my insecurities got the best of me. Paul and I were leaving the gym together, we argued, and he asked me if I still wanted to be with him. I can still remember my innards trembling as I said, "I'd prefer if we were just friends." I felt like I was completely detached from my body, like I was floating above it all, not really feeling what I was saying. I had somehow convinced myself that I was going to get on with my well-laid plans and live my measured life with Mike, who had never stopped waiting. So even in the face of a deep and clear knowing, the pull of my cautious and logical self was too strong. And just like that I lost Paul.

There was security and comfort in the plan of going back to Mike. I could deal with that—I could comprehend it. It was tangible, with clear and measurable indicators of "the right thing to do."

I truly wanted to remain friends with Paul. I wanted to continue our deep conversations and explore life's mysteries with him—all the while building life's certainties with Mike. But this option was not mine to choose. Paul's hurt was too deep and he had fallen too far to go back to the way we were:

"One day, you will want to talk to me about your primary relationship, as friends do. I won't be able to do that for you, I'm not strong enough to be around someone I love this much and pretend that this is okay." He told me not to contact him, and he set out to rebuild his own life and pretend that this had all been a delusion.

The night I recommitted to Mike, we were to meet at 8 P.M. I arrived at the restaurant early with my stomach in knots. On some level, I knew I was betraying all that I had learned about love and myself, and that I wasn't being fair to Mike, but I rationalized the knots in my stomach as nervousness about seeing an old boyfriend.

A few years prior, Mike had gifted me a watch, and as I waited, I saw the minutes tick by—7:56 P.M., 7:57 P.M., 7:58 P.M. . . . When Mike walked in, a fire moved through my core, but I still stood up and hugged him. I proceeded to tell him I was sorry I left and that it was a mistake. After our meal, we left the restaurant together. Later that night, when I looked at my watch, I was stunned to see it had stopped telling time at 7:59 P.M. It was February 2001.

CHAPTER 4

COURSE CORRECTION

———— • ————

It is late spring 2001, and I now have a temporary position as an administrative assistant at a Fortune 500 corporation. I'm not entirely sure what our division does or makes, but I have a sensible commute to a safe part of town, and they gave me my own cubicle. I am working for an engineer, entering data, and I am bored out of my mind, a level of boredom I had not known was possible. But I am making great money, and isn't that the point? Although I haven't seen or talked to Paul since the winter, he is on my mind all the time. I miss him profoundly.

It's June 14, a beautiful sunny spring day. It is lunchtime and I am having a salad with a colleague. We are talking about a car accident we heard about on the news that morning and how lucky we are these things only seem to happen to other people. Walking back to the office, a bird poops on her shoulder and we laugh out loud, saying that if this is the worst that happens, we are good.

Later that afternoon, Mike calls to say he wants to go golfing after work and has invited two friends to come along.

I feel my stomach knotting again. I do not want to go golfing with him. If anything, I want to go surfing with Paul. I dislike golfing and I miss having meaningful and life-giving experiences where you get to wholeheartedly abandon yourself to the moment and discover something new. Then in comes the rational me, the "commonsense" me. I remind myself I made a choice to be in this relationship and how compromises are part of making relationships work. Going golfing with Mike would make him happy. I say yes.

We golf, we drink a beer, and we have a few laughs with our friends. When the sun begins to go down, we head out on the oceanside road, back toward Halifax. I take in its scenic beauty as we twist and turn past bedrock cliffs, pine forests, and quaint fishing villages. It's the same road I used to take on my way to Paul's restaurant. Mike sees a gas station and decides to stop. He makes a left turn toward the station but fails to correctly judge the distance between our car and the half-ton truck coming toward us in the other lane.

I remember screaming *What the hell!* at Mike.

I remember feeling so pissed at him for making a risky turn.

I remember moving my body to the left as if I could avoid the collision with this heavy speeding object hurtling right at me.

I am fully exposed and vulnerable as the truck barrels down the road and smashes into our car.

I don't remember the car doing a 360.

I don't remember all the glass breaking and the passenger door smashing onto me.

All I remember is going in and out of consciousness.

When I regain consciousness, I can't breathe and my body hurts. And when I lose consciousness, nothing hurts, I am fine, and I have an awareness of being quite blissful. And that is when I experience a parallel life.

I am transported to a choice point, a fork in the road, each path leading to an alternate reality. I am projected through time and space and into the experience of a life that isn't my own but for a single choice: the one my heart has chosen for me, the one my mind has denied.

I feel amazing, although I remain aware I am trapped in a car. I see myself with Paul—one moment we are surfing, the next we are playing with our children, and then traveling the world. I see myself writing books and teaching. I am exuberant, peaceful, joyful. I experience unconditional love and know I am connected with everyone and everything. I love deeply and allow myself to be loved. Love itself seems to flow through my veins.

On my way back to consciousness I become aware of the contrast between the life that I am leading and the life in my vision. I am able to hold both realities in my awareness without judgment. I relive the intimacy of the summer before. Something is coming back for me, coming to bring me home.

It lasts for a few seconds, maybe minutes. The next time I regain consciousness, I try to breathe. It is difficult, but I manage to get little sips of air that seem to be keeping me awake.

All around me, people are panicked. Bystanders have stopped to help and are frantically calling on their phones and screaming out orders. Mike is in shock at the sight of me trapped in the car. My girlfriend who was a passenger in the back seat is unconscious, and we are told she isn't breathing. People think she is dead. It's chaotic and I am in pain, but I also know it will all be okay. I am not worried about dying. I am not worried about my friend, I know she will be okay. I am filled with peace.

It takes 20 minutes for the paramedics to arrive. The passenger door is inoperable, so they ease the stretcher into the car through the sunroof and remove me from the wreck through that small hole. Paramedics help me with my breathing all the way to the hospital, where I have to undergo emergency surgery.

My lungs have partially collapsed and my liver has sustained a large laceration from the impact. When the surgeons operate, they see that my liver has split in half down the middle, between the two lobes. It bled out internally, but somehow, the bleeding stopped in the ambulance on the way to the hospital. The surgeon has never seen anything like it.

I wake up in an ICU after the surgery on the morning of June 15.

I know with every single cell in my body that the life I witnessed was mine, mine to remember, mine to reclaim. It is time to stop ignoring the call in the form of a flame within myself. I promise myself if I survive, I will stop letting my fears and my cautious self have power over my deeper knowing. I realize how many details will need to change and how I need to take responsibility for who I have let myself become. I know I have to wake up to the life I was born to live and find who I truly am.

Mike had called my parents in the night, and they had decided to leave the next day and drive from Quebec. They would arrive two days later, as it was their routine to break up the trip with a night in a B&B. Although this bothers Mike, I don't give it a second thought. I pride myself on being a strong, independent person. I got that from my granny.

When I am more stable, friends come to visit. At one point, I covertly ask my friend to call Paul. She comes back from the hallway several minutes later and informs me with no explanation that he won't be coming.

There are some things we have to do on our own.

CHAPTER 5

GRANNY

———— • ————

Granny's way to show me she loved me was to let me play the slot machines at the corner store in rural Quebec. Not everyone understood our bond, but we communicated it in our own special way. She was the perfect accomplice and wasn't afraid to bend or break any of my mother's rules. In fact, she delighted in it. In addition to bringing us to other gambling activities (Bingo!), she would sneakily give my brother and me small amounts of money, candy, and other treats. This defiant behavior wasn't reserved only for her daughter, as she frequently duped her cardiologist by fibbing about her cholesterol intake. She was obsessed with seafood, and she taught me how to eat fresh lobster and crab dipped in butter on the rocky shores of Saint-Laurent.

Later in life, when she entered a retirement home, she would write me letter after letter about her mundane days where her favorite activity was to get on her adult tricycle and ride to the mailbox on the edge of the grounds to see if I had written her back. As a teenager, I didn't put as much importance on writing her back as I now wish I had.

I was 16 years old when Granny was admitted to the hospital after her third heart attack. My mother was driving to Montreal to see her and I wanted to go with her. She refused on the pretext that I shouldn't miss any school. She later told me the real reason was she didn't want to expose me to my grandmother's suffering. She wanted to protect me from pain.

So I stayed back at our cottage on the lake. I remember sitting by myself on the dock with my feet in the water, talking to Granny in my mind, telling her I hoped she felt better soon. Later that night I called the hospital to speak to her. The nurse informed me she could not come to the phone and was not allowed to answer the one in her room because of her deteriorating state. I gasped a little as I pictured her all alone in a green-gray hospital room, and I asked the nurse to tell Granny that I wished her a good night. With a gruff voice, the nurse yelled, "Your granddaughter wishes you a *bonne nuit*." I heard Granny respond, "Tell her I wish her the same." I was struck by the vitality of her voice and I still remember her words vividly.

The next morning my mother called to tell me Granny had passed in the night. My heart broke open. It was the first time I had lost someone close to me. My mother said the funeral would be the following day and that she would return after. I asked if I could come, but again, citing the need to protect me from pain, she refused. I hung up the phone, walked back to the end of the dock, and sat down. I was overwhelmed with a sense of loss and I cried out of sadness, out of anger. I was mad at my grandmother for not giving me more notice. I was mad at my mother for not letting me be there. I was mad at myself for wasting precious time when she was alive. I wished I had more time to show her how much I loved her. I felt confused and alone.

My upbringing in the Catholic Church would not help me in this moment. I wondered what my archbishop would say. What would he tell me to *do* or *think*? I couldn't relate to the explanations of the afterlife and the soul as they were described in my church. I had learned them as stories with a sense of detachment: they were mystical, entertaining, and sometimes boring. But now that I needed them the most, they didn't feel real to me. So where was my grandmother?

I couldn't imagine this person I loved and spoke to just hours ago had left completely because nothing about our relationship felt like it had really changed. Other than the fact that I was told she had died. I was expecting a dramatic occurrence, like a dark cloud coming over me and my family. But it wasn't even close to that. Facing death for the first time, I was struck by its impotence and its irrelevance. In truth, I was still her beloved granddaughter. The feeling was intact and the nature of our relationship remained untouched. To this day I still remember experiencing this knowing as the sensation of energy moving through my body. There was an understanding in my heart, reassuring me about our connection, hinting at something greater.

I sat on the dock with no one else around. I found myself yelling and crying. I held nothing back as waves of emotion ran through me. After the storm of tears, I became quiet. For a moment there was nothing, just stillness. No positive or negative emotions. Everything felt neutral.

I closed my eyes and focused on this relationship with my granny that was still very much real in me. It was she who had introduced me to prayer, whispering instructions in my ear after, as we knelt after communion. I felt as though I had been allowed into a direct conversation with God.

I went back to that timeless place of prayer in my mind and I could feel her presence again, strongly, all through and around me, more so than even when she was alive. The connection was more direct, and anything that used to be in the way was gone.

I closed my eyes and spoke out loud to her, "So, this is how it is with us now!" I could feel her reassuring me. I continued, "How are you feeling? Where are you? Do you need anything?" I felt so close to her. Not with my mind, but with my feelings and my heart. More tears came, but now they were tears of joy, and they softened my pain. I felt loved and so lucky to have this moment with her.

When I opened my eyes, a white butterfly was fluttering in front of me just above the water. Was it there for me? I quietly observed as it lingered. Did Granny have something to do with this? After a while, it flew toward the forest and I happily followed. It landed on a mossy rock and stayed there as I gathered rocks and flowers and arranged my own little funeral ceremony for my grandmother. Surrounded by nature, I was aware of her presence.

I knew after that she was not really gone. Even better, she was closer to me than ever. Her body and the emotional walls that prevented her from expressing deep tenderness were no longer limitations. There were no conditions to her love. What makes a person special is their unseen essence, their eternal self. I began to understand that the love that resides between two people has more to do with the invisible bond than with the roles they play or the things they do. My connection with Granny after she passed introduced me to a dimension of myself that felt boundless and vast.

I was only 16, and although her presence has never left me and is still strong to this day, I forgot the deeper meaning of this experience until the car accident.

CHAPTER 6

A WILD INNER KNOWING

———— • ————

W hat really happened in the moments after the accident? What caused the phenomenon of me experiencing another existence so vividly? I really didn't know. I had no frame of reference for something like that. But I remember thinking to myself, *This must be a spiritual experience—this must have something to do with my soul.* Back then, my knowledge of spiritual affairs was limited. I hadn't let much "soul" enter my well-controlled life. But from what I knew, this was a spiritual experience—mysterious, special, and important.

Then again, the key question really was: Why was it so important to me that it changed the direction of my life? I was in my early twenties. I was supposed to be trying things out, going down the wrong path, and making mistakes. Besides, people make mistakes for decades without being jarred out of their body with a mystical experience. Why me? Why now?

In the year before the accident, I knew something was off. I felt discontentment; I wasn't at peace with myself, far from it. I was always looking for something to do or plan for so I could be busy becoming who I thought I should be. Instead of addressing the unease of being in my own skin, I chose to create endless distractions. I threw myself into a myriad of activities and addictions to drown out the discomfort. I attempted to fill the void with parties, relationship drama, overplanning, controlling every aspect of my life, and being a really good student at university.

While the thought of having my future planned out with Mike was comforting and even exciting to think about some-times—the trappings of fancy properties and cars and vacations that our successful careers would bring—something inside me knew it would never really fill that feeling of empti-ness. I had a puzzling inner knowing that no matter what we accomplished or came to own, it would not be enough.

What was this knowing? I used to call it my crazy voice. It felt like a little flame and sounded like a voice coming from deep inside my being, but it wasn't my friend. I thought of it as a daydream, a feral part of myself, like a fault or an error in my genetic makeup. I didn't trust this voice, even though it was there every single day and had been with me for as long as I could remember. I ignored it most of the time, taking my cues from my common-sense thinking brain that learned from how people around me lived.

I know now that the accident happened for a reason. It wasn't my time to die. It was my time to begin to pay attention to that inner knowing that wasn't so crazy after all. In fact, I had a sense that ignoring it was more likely to drive me crazy or lead to more dramatic occurrences. The time had come to trust myself, even though I had no idea who this person was that I needed to trust.

— • —

It is two weeks after the accident and I am lying in a hospital bed. My life has come to an abrupt halt. I am weak, dependent, scared. I can't go to the washroom by myself and I really want to wash my hair, but that will have to wait.

I have nothing but time to lie here and reflect on my life. The accident gives me an awareness of the great dissonance between the two different parallel lives, one real and one remembered. Something about the mystical experience feels very familiar to me. I am brought back to those moments with my granny on the dock and the feeling of closeness and wholeness and the essence of the experience. It is undeniable to me that both my experience with Granny and the accident were peak spiritual occurrences related in some way.

The accident showed me clearly that what seems important to the people around me isn't going to bring me peace, or joy, or a sense of fulfillment. If this is true, then what is going to make me happy? What is happiness anyway? Is inner peace and fulfillment even achievable for tshe common mortal? Can I trust this wild inner knowing to lead the way? Is it sane? Is it even safe? I don't have the answers to these questions, but I have a sense that something more powerful than my human mind is leading the way.

My life with Mike was like a train on a track with its own momentum. So when I return home, my "real" life is waiting for me. Family and friends lovingly help me return to a sense of normalcy. But I am not the same.

Mike wasn't injured in the accident. Not physically, anyway. But the thought of losing me, of causing this pain, of almost killing his friends, is traumatizing for him. And he doesn't speak of it much at all. I feel for him.

I deeply want to reconnect with Paul. Perhaps he can help navigate this new reality. I want to tell him about my spiritual experience in the accident. I still miss him very much. But in the months since I last saw him, he has been building a life that doesn't include me. Weeks after I get out of the hospital, I decide to reach out again. I send him a couple of pleasant texts. He is still very hurt, angry, and hesitant to trust me. He confirms, in no uncertain terms, that he has no desire to pursue a friendship with me. I can't blame him.

I'm leaving for Ontario. Can I see you before I go?

Please Fuck Off

I tell myself if I am to ever connect with him again, it won't be until I work on dealing with my own baggage, because under no circumstances would I ever again want to put him through pain. Although we are estranged, he is my very favorite person in the world. He is the last person I want to hurt. I suspect if I have any hope of navigating a love like that, I will have to get my act together and work on myself first.

So my first step is to remove myself from my habitual surroundings. I need a big pattern interruption so I cannot fall back into old ones. I need new surroundings and new people in my life to help me stay true to what I deeply know.

So I move 1,700 kilometers away to Ontario and begin my education degree.

CHAPTER 7

DISPLACEMENT

———— • ————

I arrive in Kingston, Ontario, in September 2001. I have moved 20 times since the age of 17. Still recovering, I feel broken, weak, and alone. Here I am again, without solid ground to walk on. I am excited for the freedom and novelty of a new place, but at the same time, I am still fragile from my insides being scrambled only two months prior. I have a desire for adventure, and when asked where I would like to do my teaching practicum next spring, I write down: *California.*

I have an appointment with the placement director at 10 A.M. to discuss the details of my international placement. As I enter his office, he is staring at the computer screen intensely. He doesn't acknowledge my presence, so I proceed to tell him about my school wish lists in California. Then he looks at me and says, "You don't know yet, do you?" He turns his computer screen toward me, and that is when I see the image of the twin towers on fire.

I walk outside to the garden area, where many students are sitting, talking, crying. Even though we are in Canada and nowhere near New York City, I feel like I am going through a fight-or-flight response.

That morning the world didn't feel safe, and it didn't for a long time after that.

CHAPTER 8

SUMMER READING

———— • ————

We don't think of summer as being a time to face our fears, but during the summer of 2002, I faced one of mine.

For the first time ever, I found myself living alone. I sublet an entire house from an older lady who insisted the house stay furnished. The original wallpaper was from 1950, the appliances were either mint green or cream yellow, and the furniture was wrapped in plastic. But it was cozy and I loved it! For the first time since junior high, I was without a serious relationship. At 24, I began to go out on dates with myself: movies, dinner, or just staying in on a Saturday night. These were my very first steps in embracing solitude.

Contemporary French writers were my favorite at the time: Ying Chen, Hélène Monette, Élise Turcotte, François Cheng. Reading their work gave me glimpses into the existential discontentment that seemed so prevalent in our modern society. They spoke directly to the drive to find meaning and the unease that lived in my own being. They knew something profound about life, but they weren't saying it directly. They were using metaphors and analogies, storytelling, and symbols, yet they were clearly working through their own understanding of life and their place in it as creative individuals.

I also began reading spiritual books. In moments of great solitude, I'd remember Paul and our conversations, and I'd find myself at the local bookstore picking up books like *The Celestine Vision* and *We Are Eternal*. In that way, I stayed close to Paul and my soul. On the advice in *The Celestine Vision*, I began to intentionally quiet my mind before I fell asleep at night, focusing my attention on my breath and enjoying the feelings relaxation brought. It would last for a minute or two before my mind came back online or I fell asleep. The feeling reminded me of prayer and praying after communion with my granny. And it was the very beginning of my meditation practice.

Although I loved my sacred evening practice, my days were very much lived in my mind, and *thinking* and *doing* were my default way.

September arrived and I returned to school, but this time as a teacher. I was hired right out of university by a prestigious private school to teach French to grades 5–6 and 7. I will always remember that first day at my first "real" job. My classroom was all set up and ready to receive students. I was walking from the teacher's lounge with a coffee in my hand. I approached the door to the classroom and stepped in. The kids were sitting in their chairs, gazing up at me. They were so beautiful, and I fell in love with them right in that moment. And in the same instant, I felt the familiar fire in my abdomen, talking to me, burning. Even though I was excited to get to know these gorgeous little humans, I knew, without a shadow of a doubt, that this career as an elementary school teacher was not for me. It was someone else's dream. I knew it because I recognized the feeling in my body, the feeling of not being in the right place.

I'd always looked up to my teachers and coaches, and my new soul compass seemed to be pointing me in the direction of teaching. Being a schoolteacher was sensible and offered a financially secure future. I remember my mom telling me it was the best job in the world—she would have done it if her life had been different. She admired and looked up to teachers, and I wanted her to admire and look up to me in the same way.

I returned to my apartment that night, disappointed and angry with myself. Why couldn't I be happy, after all the time and effort I put into getting here? I was fully aware that for many of my friends and family, this would be a dream job. But I knew better than to ignore this feeling in my belly. I had learned this was my soul telling me something important, and I needed to listen.

I promised myself I would do the very best job I could that year for these kids. And I did. But I also applied right away to do my master's degree in contemporary French literature, and by November, I had been accepted for the next year. I greatly desired to ponder things deeply and figure out the meaning of life. I wasn't finished being a student. Studying literature at a graduate level seemed the best way to do that.

The question then became: If I was not an elementary school teacher, was I a university professor?

CHAPTER 9

BEYOND THE BREAK

·

Surf's up at Lawrencetown

This wasn't quite the open-armed invitation I was hoping for, but it would have to do. I'd never had to court men before, and it showed. Two and a half years after, I'd finally managed to strike an e-mail tone that was the right mix of polite and platonic to keep Paul from reporting me as spam.

During these past years, Paul was constantly in my awareness. Even though this process of finding myself and getting closer to my own heart was ultimately my own journey and was separate from the one back to Paul, deep down inside I knew our destinies were interwoven and would unlock a life I couldn't even imagine. Our paths would cross in my mind and in my imagination when I'd read a great book or when I felt inspired by a project. He was part of my inner world and I would talk about him to friends. He became this character in my story, although he wasn't aware of it. But I did send him birthday cards, left messages at his work, and even tried to surprise him with an ill-fated Christmas trip to Nova Scotia. I say ill-fated because a) he didn't want to see me, b) he was in Cuba with his girlfriend, and c) I ended up with food poisoning.

Not to be deterred, I persisted. Through an e-mail exchange, I had come to suspect that things were less than perfect with his on-again, off-again girlfriend. Was this enough of an opening to justify a second 3,000-kilometer round-trip drive to Halifax? It's hard to say, but again, I didn't have much experience with courting boys. It was a long shot, but my best friend, Elsa, and I hopped into my Toyota Echo and made the drive.

Despite my persistence, Paul was unwilling to lie or risk a fight with his girlfriend. He wouldn't agree to meet me. So when he e-mailed *Surf's up at Lawrencetown*, his choice of words spoke to his ambiguity toward me. It was crystal clear this was not a date. It's not like he gave me a time or a location. And with Lawrencetown being Nova Scotia's busiest surf beach, the chance of finding him in the crowd was pretty slim.

I recruited another friend and the three of us headed out to the beach. When I caught that first glimpse of him walking up over the sand dune with his surfboard, it felt utterly right, and at the same time, completely surreal. To have such confirmation that I was in the right place at the right time was a magnificent feeling. But don't worry, I played it cool.

Everyone was polite and cordial, and Paul's manners made him hard to read, especially if he didn't want to be read. We put on our wetsuits and he gave my friends a quick surf lesson. I was nervous I might come on too strong, but eventually the two of us slowly drifted away from the crowd, sitting quietly on our boards in the calm water behind the surf. There were about 300 people at the beach that day, clear skies, and lots of surfers in the water. But as we talked and drifted, a cocooning haze surrounded us. As we faced each other, time slowed down, and everyone else seemed to disappear. We were literally alone in the huge sea, and for the first time in almost three years, I was able to look into his eyes.

"We should be together, you know. Don't you want to be happy?" I asked.

"I don't care about being happy. I want meaning in my life."

I wasn't prepared for that. "Do you feel you can have that with me?"

He didn't answer.

In that moment, on the surfboards in the middle of the calm sea, Paul echoed that wild inner knowing within myself. The way that I understood life shifted in an instant. This was a peak experience. I remembered the full extent of my spiritual essence, and happiness was the outcome of that meaning. And I knew without a shadow of a doubt I could be on that path with Paul. I knew he would value my journey for meaning and self-realization and support me. I wanted him to be the one with whom I shared this journey. And I wanted to be part of all that was meaningful to him.

That evening we met up with friends at a bar. It was difficult to talk, so we snuck out to his car and hid there for hours, talking. I knew there was no turning back. He confided the past three years had been very difficult, that losing me was one of the hardest things he had ever gone through. He'd had a difficult time keeping it together at work, had struggled with depression, and hadn't been able to invest himself in any other relationship.

I left Nova Scotia in love. In love with my life, with my path, with my questions, my confusion, and my desires. I left Nova Scotia in love with Paul. He was no longer a fantasy or a delusion.

One month later, after my master's program began, I flew back to visit Paul. He had rented a cottage by the ocean, and that evening, as the sky was dramatically changing colors and the wind was picking up, we went snorkeling in the rising tide.

Floating atop the troubled waters, I watch him dive down deep into the dark and cold water of the Atlantic Ocean, looking for lobster. As Hurricane Juan touched land, we were warm and cozy inside by the fire, eating dinner, renewing our commitment to each other. We decided then that Paul would come stay with me in Kingston, at least for the length of my program.

Weeks later, he pulled into my driveway with his Toyota filled to the brim. One of the first things he said to me was, "Do you know that tomorrow is Soulmate Day?" Somehow he convinced me this was a real thing, some sort of English Hallmark holiday, and he spent the day showering me with gifts and poems. We went for a long walk and had a candlelit dinner at Le Chien Noir in the old part of the city. When we came back home, there were rose petals all over the room. When I turned around, he was down on one knee. Somehow I hadn't seen it coming. To this day we still celebrate Soulmate Day, and it definitely beats all the other English culture Hallmark holidays.

I got all the things I thought I wanted, but my life wasn't through evolving. Not even close.

CHAPTER 10

TWO YEARS, TWO CONTINENTS, TWO DEGREES, AND A BABY

From the outside looking in, my life was picture-perfect. I was newly engaged to the man I wanted to spend the rest of my life with. I was completing my master's degree under a thesis director I highly admired. And I had been accepted to do my Ph.D. in Bordeaux, France. At the end of the year, we moved back to Nova Scotia, where Paul's restaurant thrived and gained renown across the province. We bought a little 100-year-old Cape Cod house close by, and shortly thereafter we found out I was pregnant. Although I would still get to go to France for courses, research, and conferences, I was granted permission to write most of my thesis from Canada. Everything happened so fast, it was as if the universe had been on hold for a while and our destiny came rushing back in now that we were together. I was on top of the world, except for one little problem.

Pain.

It began when I was teaching. I'd get sinus infections every time I'd have a cold or the flu. They would go away with medication, but then, when I began doing my master's, the pain would subtly appear on rainy days, a dull buzz all around my eyes. It would not last too long, drying up with the sun. It was when we moved back to Nova Scotia, the rainiest place I knew, except for Kauai, that the pain began to establish itself more permanently. I was pregnant, trying to finalize my dissertation, and dealing with chronic pain in my head—a heaviness, like a blanket of fog, that didn't allow me to see clearly or focus.

The pain was subtle at first. In some ways, that made it easier to ignore at the beginning. I had all kinds of rational explanations for it—allergies, a virus, fatigue—and I even wondered if it was "all in my head." Antibiotics sometimes did the trick, but then on the next gray, rainy day, the pain snuck in again, stronger than before. Increasingly, when the sun came out, the pain didn't disappear. It just stayed there, nagging, annoying, and slowly chipping away at my patience. Soon, the pain was present every morning when I woke up. It was chronic, it was constant, and it never took a break. I looked for distractions, thinking it would go away if I didn't think about it. But there was nowhere to go.

My head, the home of my intellect and the part of myself I valued the most, was not working properly. Up until then, my ability to focus and get things done was central to my identity and self-worth. It was the only way I knew how to be "me." My intelligent mind had been on my side for so long, and now, when I was writing my thesis and needed it the most, it was failing me. The pain slowly took away my joie de vivre. It was difficult to find joy and meaning, because during that time in my life, joy and meaning came from what I *thought* and what I *did*.

I told myself that the pain had likely been aggravated by my pregnancy and therefore would likely go away after I gave birth. But then Olivier arrived in February 2005, born without a cry and not breathing. The doctors made him breathe very quickly and pinged his little toes to make him cry a little. He made a tiny squeak and returned to being silent, with his eyes wide open. The doctors wrapped him in a blanket and placed him on my lap. I bent my knees up so I could see him better, making his eyes level with mine.

I stared at him in awe. So much chaos had just happened. First the pain of the birth, and then the loud voices and noises of the hospital staff responding to a baby not breathing. But when I looked into Olivier's eyes, he was a little being who was completely unaffected by any of this external storm. He was at peace. He was peace. And in the simplicity of this peace there was tremendous joy. I saw in him Divine love. I was there, present with him, present with Paul, and I thought, *This is the feeling I had in the accident. This is who I am. This is who we are.* I shed tears of joy.

Olivier was an easy baby. He was content to simply *be* in his body in this life, on this earth, at this time. If something was wrong in his world, he had a distinct cry we could easily attribute to needing a diaper change or food. But most of the time, life was giving him enough. What a gift he was to the world. What a gift he was to me.

Unfortunately, the pain in my head exploded after his birth. Something in me awakened the night Olivier was born. With his spirit shining through his eyes, Olivier broke my heart wide open, bringing peace and joy, and lighting up a very different path. One where *thinking* and *doing* took a backseat to *feeling* and *being*. It was abundantly clear my well-laid plans were not flexible enough for what my heart desired. Trying to fit this expanded awareness back into my life created more pressure in my body, more pain in my head. My physical and emotional bodies were yelling even louder, demanding I pay attention.

I saw my family doctor. She referred me to an allergist and a radiologist. They couldn't find anything wrong with me. She prescribed me nasal sprays, more antibiotics, and painkillers. The problem still didn't go away. I veered away from traditional medicine and started to see a chiropractor and a naturopath. I took supplements, I changed my diet, and I began to do yoga. All of these things helped a little, softening the edges of the pain, only to feel it return a day or two later.

I began to see a lovely massage therapist who was an incredible Reiki healer. During these sessions I would feel enveloped in a warm blanket of love and safety. Afterward, I always noticed my spirits had been lifted and I was less gloomy. But still, every morning when I woke up, the pain was there. After a full year of seeing her regularly, she said, "Anne, some things you just have to learn to live with." I was devastated.

Using my mind to think, write, and strategize is what I *did*. I couldn't do that with a thinking apparatus that hurt all the time. I was close to the end of my rope, defeated. Deep down inside of me, a voice said, "This is not something you have to live with. Your life does not have to be defined by pain." The only problem was I didn't know what else to try, nor did I have any idea where to turn next.

When Olivier turned one year old, I was battling low-grade postpartum depression and I was trying to keep it at bay and convince myself it wasn't happening, that I was happy, but I was sad all the time. I remember a few weeks went by with me crying every single day. I hadn't experienced sadness like that before. It almost felt like it was for no reason—at least no reason I could understand or make sense of.

What made it worse was that I had this habitual routine that didn't help at all. After I'd put Olivier to bed early in the evening, I'd open a bottle of wine. Paul would come home late from working in the restaurant, and I'd already be halfway through the bottle. I didn't want him to see my dark side, and the wine seemed to mask my real mood. It also took the edge off the pain.

After months of this behavior, when I had a checkup with my family doctor, she asked me to fill out a questionnaire. I now know that these questionnaires come out in postpartum to identify and help new mothers dealing with baby blues or depression. One of the questions was "How many drinks do you have per week?" Being in the fine dining industry, there really wasn't a night we didn't drink. I hadn't realized how much I was drinking until I had to tally the drinks per week!

That night I didn't drink, and when Paul came home, I talked to him. I shared with him that I had been feeling sad and weepy for a while now. I felt ashamed of not being able to handle my life. I felt like I wasn't being a good mom, a good wife, a good mother. I was disappointed in myself. The plans I had made and wanted to follow through with were on hold because of this pain and because of this sadness. I didn't tell Paul all these feelings. I simply told him I wasn't sure why I was sad.

I'll always remember his response. He began to share with me how he'd gone through depression when he was a teenager and how he'd gone to some pretty dark places himself. He said, "It's okay to accept that you're depressed. If you resist the feeling, it will only feed the problem. Be okay with being sad and not knowing why."

I took a deep breath, and on the exhalation, I wept in his arms. This was such a foreign feeling. I didn't love it, but at least I wasn't alone anymore.

CHAPTER 11

WHERE'S THE EXIT?

———— • ————

I didn't understand exactly what the day would be about, but the title lured me in. It was called Women in Leadership, it was being presented by the WEL-Systems Institute, and it pleased my ego. I felt privileged to be invited and to be considered a leader in some way. In Teachers College, my degree focus was leadership and I did my practicum shadowing a principal in a private school in California. I thought I would one day be a principal, the "leader" of the teachers!

Being a leader had always come naturally. Even as a child, I'd been the one organizing races and directing plays and variety shows with the other kids in my neighborhood. There is a recording of me bossing my brother around when I was five and he was two, saying, "Toro, Toro," and then demanding he run through my red blanket like a bull. I wanted to learn more about this leadership thing and how I could apply it in my career. Little did I know that this particular workshop had nothing to do with the kind of leadership I was familiar with. In fact, if I'd known what would really happen that day, I never would have gone.

The facilitator, Louise LeBrun, began the day talking about a very different type of leadership than the one I was familiar with and expecting. I was immediately annoyed. She spoke of a type of leadership that comes from within and allows us to reconnect with a deep innate knowing that lives in the cells of our body. This kind of leadership was based in the creative, organic, and sacred way women are naturally designed to lead. It drew on the gifts and the sensitivities of the feminine. It required us to be very much in touch with our vulnerability and our emotions.

As she was speaking, some women around me began to cry. I was horrified. In my mind, these kinds of emotional displays were reserved for when you are in private or with a friend you trust. But these women didn't seem to mind being vulnerable in front of people they didn't know. And their tears didn't faze Louise either. She simply incorporated the importance of communicating authentic emotions into the conversation.

My irritation grew and my mind was racing. I hadn't signed up for this. I looked around the room for the exit door so I could excuse myself, but there never seemed to be a natural break in the conversation. I didn't want to be there, let alone listen. But my social conditioning included deep-seated rules about interrupting the teacher, so I stayed. I sat there quietly angry, quietly annoyed, with the pressure in my body rising, especially in my head. I felt as if it would explode.

As if she knew this was happening, Louise began talking about the importance of being true to what we feel in the present moment and breathing deeply into that feeling. She spoke of remembering the true leader we are, not from our intellect, but from a place deep within the body. She spoke of the importance of being honest with ourselves and allowing the truth of the hurt of the past we carry to be seen and processed in the body. Breath was the key to this process.

While my mind was in full-on revolt, my heart was listening very attentively and soaking up every single word. It wanted its turn to lead and suddenly seized the opportunity. The pressure and pain in my head reached a pinnacle. Usually, if I felt like that, I would hold my breath, swallow a couple of times, and leave the room. I didn't have the option to leave, so I held my breath, but it only made the pressure more intense. All this talk about breathing made me do something next that was completely counterintuitive.

I took a deep breath.

This caused a rock to form in my throat. And it felt like it was on fire. I couldn't swallow. I struggled to take another deep breath, and this time, the breath sounded like a strange animal was dying. The passage of air through my throat was growing more restricted, and I panicked as I had the night of the accident when my lungs weren't working. This panic quickly deepened and I felt like I was reliving an event I couldn't remember. I was scared and helpless.

Louise came over and began to guide me in my breathing, encouraging me to deepen it. She didn't seem too concerned about the fact that I couldn't breathe. Louise had a grounded presence and reassuring eyes. She wasn't trying to control any part of this experience. She just *was* with me. With her guidance to trust myself and my ability to move through whatever this was, I took the next breath. Taking that breath felt like irrational courage and crazy surrender. It felt as if I was falling backward into the arms of my own heart, having no choice but to trust I would somehow catch myself.

With that breath, tears that I had no control over and that came from deep within rushed through me. I had never experienced anything like this because I would not have let myself get this far, this "out of control." My heart had taken over my being, and I found myself in a big hot mess of snot and strange weeping sounds. It was neither pretty, dainty, nor graceful.

Not the kind of thing I would *ever* do in public in front of people I didn't fully know. But there I was, emotionally naked and vulnerable. My body shook and trembled. I felt hot, then numb, then cold.

After a few minutes, my body stabilized and I felt calm.

I had the sense a huge weight had been lifted from my throat and head. My body felt light, and I was filled with an incredible sense of peace that stayed with me for weeks after. I could breathe better than ever before.

I realized that day how much shame I held around showing vulnerability and expressing emotions. Most importantly, I discovered how controlling all aspects of me and of my life, including the emotional side, had kept me from feeling that shame and the suppressed emotions that lived in me. These suppressed emotions were controlling me, keeping me from feeling free in my being. But now they had been shown the escape hatch.

It was the very first time I gave my emotions attention at such a deep level—I was completely blindsided. I had no idea these emotions lived in my inner body and that trying to figure them out with my mind was not really healing. I didn't know my physical health was connected to my emotions. I knew when I was really sad or upset about something for a sustained amount of time, I tended to get sick. But what I discovered was that I had built up layers and layers of experiences inside my body that were unexamined, unprocessed, and creating tremendous pressure.

CHAPTER 12

FINDING MOTHER

———— • ————

" **I**f it's a girl, I'm going to throw her in the garbage."
My mother's labor had been hard; she had wanted to jump out the window into the dark, snowy January night. But, of course, people don't mean everything they say when they are in labor. And as soon as I was born, she felt this pride in me and wanted to protect me from the world. She called me her precious ray of sun. In her own way, she loved me, as much as she could.

But looking back, I believe in that moment, my mother had revealed a truth that lurked in the shadows of our family's ancestry. Something unspoken had been passed through the generations—a belief, as subtle as a single thread in a tapestry, yet as potent as a mutated gene smuggled in on our DNA.

Meanwhile, I was born with the umbilical cord around my neck, unable to scream. It was the winter of 1978.

When did this suffering begin? What was the original injury that could leave a woman not wanting a girl? I didn't know my great-grandmother, but my grandmother may have offered some clues. Granny was a tomboy who coached hockey and never really wanted to have kids, and certainly not girls. Nevertheless, she had three daughters and two sons. She didn't seem to have a natural instinct for nurturing and tenderness. She had an incredible mind, but dinner was often an unopened can of corn dropped on the table as she ran out the door to a game or practice. I was told she suffered greatly from sinus pain. I was told she wasn't the unconditionally loving type. This would color my mother's understanding of love.

When I think about my own relationship with femininity, I can see hints of that mysterious thread from the very beginning of my life. As a little girl, my mother dressed me more in boys' clothes and kept my hair short. I didn't have girlfriends with whom I could have played dolls or talk about boys. In fact, my very best friend growing up was a boy named Nicolas. Although I didn't know it then, Nicolas was gay. Neither of us saw the other as an object of desire, and we were free of gender roles and expectations as we played in the forest, gathering moss, climbing trees, and talking to fairies in the rain.

When I was 11, we moved to an asbestos mining town and I had to leave Nicolas and my forest behind. The reality of being a preteen came rushing in with all the forms it usually takes. Romantic relationships were a foreign language I didn't care to learn. I had very few female friends. I couldn't relate to their priorities or interests. However, thanks to being good at sports, I was able to position myself as being "one of the guys."

I really hated having my period. It was nothing more than an unwelcome drain on my athletic performance. I wanted my body to be able to do what I wanted it to do when I wanted it to do it. The emotional aspect may have been the worst. For one week, once a month, I wasn't able to control my thoughts, my words, or my mood. I would become someone I hated. I resented being a girl.

Fast-forward to age 26. I was on the cusp of a new shift in identity, about to become a mother and a wife in the same year. Life had once again blessed me with the knowledge that I had very little of it figured out. As I partook in the miracle of making a human being, I resisted every part of it. I didn't want my life to change, but there I was, vomiting every single day with my productivity thrown out the window. My fear was if I was "like a woman," I would lose my ability to get things *done*, to accomplish what I wanted to accomplish. I had a deep fear of losing complete control of my life.

What kind of mother or matriarch would I be? By the time my son was one, I realized my emotional unavailability wasn't a healthy way to raise a child. Olivier loved the adventure of life. It was inspiring to witness how free and exuberant he was in the expression of his emotions, how close he was to his desires and his needs—a gorgeous soul, expressing his life force with no inhibitions. When he was sad or upset, he simply cried. When he cried, I felt my body tighten and close up. I would become impatient, sometimes even angry. I wanted to shield him from that energy of impatience and anger—obviously he had nothing to do with this; the issue was all mine. I didn't want to project that onto him, but I didn't want to bottle it up either. I knew there was more in me to be addressed, and I wanted to do the emotional work for my sake and his. So I headed off to another workshop with Louise.

It was a five-day workshop, and I was ready that week to go deep. I trusted my mentor and knew I had a lot of emotional baggage from my past. I committed to keeping my mind and heart open throughout the whole week. As I sat there breathing deeply with my awareness within, wave after wave of healing came through me, releasing old, dead beliefs, most of which were tied up in childhood events. I had never been aware of my inner body like this before. Sitting there in the group, I was aware of the noises my stomach was making. The more attention and breath I brought to that area, the louder the rumblings became. It was as if my inner belly had been ignored for so long that now that I was paying attention to it, it was excited to tell me everything it had wanted to tell me for a long time.

Eventually, the rumbling eased, but I kept breathing deeply with my attention on my lower body. There was excitement communicated to me, but there was also sadness. I felt the movement of gas in my intestines. I felt butterflies in my stomach for no apparent reason. I felt heat; I felt energy. It was a kinesthetic experience, yet it felt incredibly sacred and loving. I had a feeling of being fully alive in my core, and I wasn't controlling the experience in any way except by being present with it, the way Louise had been present with me in the previous workshop. It was me just *being* me, and the sensations and movements were happening on their own.

Through this experience with my belly, both of my parents came into my awareness. At the time, our relationship, especially with my mother, was strained. When I left the house at 17, I was ready to break free from what I felt was too much control. I had purposefully chosen a school program that was not offered in my town, far enough away that I would need to move out on my own. It was difficult to come back and visit with them because each time would end in a fight. I didn't want our relationship to be like that. I wanted to enjoy them and them to enjoy me.

We were halfway through the workshop and were talking about family dynamics and the legacy of authority figures in the wiring of our bodies when painful knots began to form in my stomach. When asked to share, I tried speaking but couldn't. Even if I could have formed words, I am not sure what I would have said—I felt like I was in a story with no content. My body was communicating, though. I brought my attention to the pain in my belly, took a deep breath, and tried to allow my body to do the work. Lots of energy moved through and out of me, accompanied by tears and trembling.

I had touched on something big and I felt the need to address it all. When we broke for lunch, I excused myself from the group and went down to a small cottage by the ocean where I knew no one could hear me. My belly was on fire. Something needed to come out.

Sitting alone in the little cottage, I began to have a conversation with my mother, the first person to come to my mind. I spoke to her out loud, even though she wasn't there. And I spoke in French, my mother tongue, the language I used when my early childhood experiences were wired in my body.

I imagined my mother standing in front of me across the room. I spoke to her as an equal and I expressed my love for her, as well as all the anger and sadness I held inside regarding our relationship. It felt strange and petty, and my mouth, my jaw, my throat, my neck, and my belly were very tense and tight. So much had been left unsaid throughout my life, and I would never say those things to her in person, but I had to give it a try. The more I opened up, the more information would come to the surface, not as thoughts but more as memories in the form of images or emotions. I would receive them, feel them, speak them, and let my body do the rest.

Anger turned into sadness, sadness turned into surrender, surrender turned into acceptance, and acceptance turned into compassion. Every layer exposed another memory, and I spoke out loud to it. I tried to stay close to the feeling of the emotions and not get into my rational mind or the story about the emotion. I kept my awareness and my breath very close to the sensations in my lower body, knowing they were the key to this process, to my healing. Eventually, the process would reveal things that had long ago faded from my conscious memory.

As these layers revealed themselves and faded away, I listened to my voice morph into that of a teenager and eventually a child. The further I was immersed in the experience of childhood, the more raw, vulnerable, and unfiltered my voice became. The words, too, became childlike, simple, and honest. At times, my voice would tremble, as the little girl inside of me would ask for what she wanted: attention, to be seen, to be acknowledged, to be validated, to feel like she mattered.

"Tu me vois? Est-ce que tu me vois? Je suis là. Embrasse moi, sert moi dans tes bras. Je veux que tu sois là, je te veux. J'ai besoin de toi."[2]

I could feel tension in my jaw and fire in my throat. It became more and more difficult to speak the words that had been repressed for so long. With deep breaths, I felt energy spreading through my face, lips, ears, jaws, head, throat, and neck. I felt my face and lips go numb. Heat flowed out of the top of my head and cold came rushing down through my body like a waterfall. It felt like energy was reshaping my body, my very flesh, with its movement.

As I continued to go back in time, I became aware of the moment when I began addressing my mother by her first name. I was six, and my younger brother and I were planning on putting on a little variety show for guests who were coming for dinner. We always entertained guests when they came to the house with singing shows and plays. We wanted our mother's help with something. Loud and excited, we were relentless in our attempts to get her attention, calling, *"Maman, Maman, Maman, Maman, Maman!"* nonstop, as kids do when they want the attention of an adult.

Likely overwhelmed with the pressures of preparing the house for her dinner guests, she lost her temper. She put her hands around my neck and yelled, "Settle down and stop calling me Maman!" When she regained her composure, she calmly asked that from now on, my brother and I call her by her first name.

I can't blame my mother for reacting in the way she did. She was confronted with emotions she didn't understand.

Later, she would celebrate this new policy as being a good thing and rather progressive. She wanted us to be independent and autonomous, and changing what we called her might help in defining a more equal relationship. It was the era of raising kids as independent little adults, and she did what she thought was best.

In the cottage that day, trying to speak the word *Maman* was like trying to pass barbed wire through my throat. It was excruciating. The word would catch on the roof of my mouth and choke me. I continued to breathe deeply, with my breath anchored deep inside my belly, and said the word *Maman* until I felt strong and grounded in saying it. I was reclaiming it as a need that had never left me: the need for closeness, affection, emotional safety, relevance, attention, and the need to be seen and heard.

I continued back in time to when my mother held me in her arms as a baby. I experienced, in my present adult body, the *feeling* of being held and nurtured by her. More tears came, although this time they were tears of joy, of love, and of tenderness. Another wave of rushing water moved through my entire body as if to reshape my flesh and integrate into my nervous system a deep remembering that I am loved, that I am supported, that I am enough, that I am safe. This was Maman. I had found her in me.

After all this, I fell asleep. When I woke up, I felt like I was arising from a dream as a new person. My body felt different—more grounded and lighter. My mind felt clear and my heart felt at peace. I felt tremendous love and compassion for my mother.

To my delight, at the end of the weeklong workshop, my sinus pain was gone for good. It was never really about the sinuses. It was all about the unresolved emotions and memories, and my sinuses were a vehicle, an outward expression trying to communicate that to me.

Now that the chronic pain is gone, I view occasional sensations in my sinus area as a gift, like a spiritual barometer. Light tingling is a signal that I am resisting change or holding on to emotions and holding on too tight to something that is not really mine. When that happens, I remind myself to breathe, let go of control, surrender and release, and stop resisting the emotions that are brought on by the changes ahead.

One of the most beautiful things to come from this experience came in the form of a phone conversation with my mother days after. She had changed! It was as though I was speaking to a whole new person, as though she had been in the cottage with me, healing too. As I listened to her, I noticed I didn't feel controlled or triggered by her. Could we be that connected? Could the work I did that day affect her, 1,200 kilometers away?

What happened in the cottage had changed aspects of her that lived inside of me—aspects of that relationship that no longer served me. I had changed my inner reality, and my outer reality followed suit. I feel such love and compassion for my mother today. We have an incredible relationship and we support each other on our paths.

CHAPTER 13

WINE-AND-CHEESE THESIS

———— • ————

S hortly after the workshop and my conversation with my mother in the cottage, I went back to the computer to continue to write my thesis. My sinus pain was no longer an issue. However, I faced a new problem: disengagement. I was no longer interested in what I was writing about. At all! Which was hard to accept, especially after having put many years into it.

Originally, on the advice of my thesis director, I had chosen a topic that made strategic sense in the context of my desire to one day be a professor. There were topics that had better chances of leading to a position. But now I had something else to share. I didn't know exactly what it was yet, but I knew it wasn't what I had been writing about. It became clear if I tried to squeeze my writing—my self—back into the box of academia the way I'd done it previously, I would risk another bout with sinus pain. I could feel that. My body had shown me what pure creativity and flow felt like, and now I wanted more.

So I took a break from writing the thesis for a few months and began a practice of just *being*. I practiced *feeling* what it meant to *be* in my body and refamiliarized myself with this biological instrument, which until now had mostly been used as a vehicle to carry my head around. It was a radical practice: just *being* with my emotions, my inner body, and the sensation of energy moving in me.

My son, Olivier, was a great teacher. He was a pro at just *being*, then *feeling* and expressing whatever came up without filtering it—he just let it flow through him. He didn't have to try, it was how he was naturally. Simply *being* with him in silence and following him around the house and outside in nature and seeing where his heart led him without controlling the experience was even more healing for me. I breathed deeply into the joy I felt inside seeing him discover the world in awe, with all his questions. I breathed deeply into the longing I held in my body to *be* that beautiful simplicity.

In the next few months, I spent a lot of time *being* and *feeling*. I wanted *being* and *feeling* in the present moment to become a way of living, not just in the workshops. I thought if I lived like that, there would be no limits to how much peace and joy I could experience. And I would rediscover who I used to be before all the inhibitions set in. Spending time with Olivier was wonderful, but I also made sure to spend time alone. I hired a babysitter a few days a week so I could practice the art of just being. Financially, I was able to afford it because in a synchronistic twist, I had received a settlement from the car accident.

With all this time by myself, I began to notice the judgmental tone of my own thoughts. I had never noticed that I criticized people and myself so harshly in my own mind. It was constant. So I began to change the dialogue a bit. For every judgment I was making toward another person, I'd change the pronoun *they* or their name for *I*. In this way, I would turn the judgment around on myself to expand its context to include me as well. For example, if I thought, *This person is being so dishonest*, I would change it to, *I am dishonest*, and I would look at my life to find ways that I was dishonest, either with others or myself. I wouldn't be critical of myself, but I would look at it with curiosity and in the spirit of releasing that judgment within me. I explored where my blind spots were and where I had limiting thought patterns in my shadow, or my unconscious. After a while, the judgmental voices quieted down.

During this period of time, I would sit down, breathe, and see what my body had to say to me. I listened with patience and tenderness. And whatever I felt inspired or called to do, I would let myself. Most of the time, it was a creative activity like painting or poetry writing. Other times, I'd realize how tired I had become and sleep.

It wasn't easy to allow myself this gift of time and space. I felt guilty about being unproductive, especially as a new mom and a Ph.D. student. But I had a strong feeling it was essential if I were to fully live as my soul's version of me that I experienced the night of the car accident. I also knew that given my driven Capricorn personality, this wouldn't go on forever.

After a few months of simply *being* present to my body and its emotions and sensations, it was time to get back to my thesis. I was about three quarters of the way through, and I really did want to finish. I still wanted to be a professor. But my months of quiet contemplation and listening within had made it abundantly clear I could no longer invest in something I didn't feel passionate about.

All of the writing I had done to this point was powered by my intellect and self-discipline. I was in uncharted waters now, and my body and heart seemed to have a different opinion about which direction this project was going to take. It was an interesting realization. No matter what my mind wanted, if my body and heart had another agenda, it couldn't be ignored.

A very loud and persuasive voice, my intellect, was demanding that I come to my senses: stay the course, put my head down, focus on the work, and finish the way I started. It was, after all, ultimately possible. But I knew I would pay a price. I knew the pain in my sinus would come back and this newfound inner peace and joie de vivre would be replaced with the physical manifestation of stress and anxiety. I wasn't willing to risk it.

I decided to look at the literature I was studying from a completely different perspective. I deeply loved the author Ying Chen and her books. I wanted to tap into my love and passion for her life and the life of her characters. I could no longer feign interest in the abstract theories that allegedly decode the work of this wonderful artist.

Ying Chen writes with introspection and an incredible sensitivity to the subtleties of art and spirit. Her characters seem to know a secret of life: they are able to create reality through their wishes and desires. Sometimes they create realities they enjoy, and sometimes they find themselves in a dead end or worse. I was curious about that process, so I decided to let that inspiration lead my writing for the final quarter of my thesis. I shifted my lens from a completely literary approach to an approach based in self-realization. I looked at her work through the lens of *autopoiesis*, a word that has both biological and literary roots.

This was a new concept and a new way of looking at Ying Chen's work that had never been done before. It was a risk, but I was inspired. I had no way of knowing how it would be received by my director or the committee that would ultimately accept or reject my bid to earn my Ph.D.

Our daughter, Hanalei, was born four months before I defended my thesis. She came into this world on the opposite side of the zodiac from our son. If Olivier was my moon, Hanalei was my sun. The night she came, she made her arrival known loud and clear to all present. Holding in my arms this fiery force of a soul, I knew she would be a very different kind of teacher to me. Accompanied by her strong "I am here" energy, I finished my dissertation.

At the University of Bordeaux, it is customary for the student to provide refreshments for the committee at her thesis defense. This was news to me, a tidbit of information shared by a secretary on the day of my defense. Paul and I scrambled to put together a spread that would be worthy of the occasion. We set up our little buffet and Paul slipped out the back door to distract our infant daughter while I waited to face the music. As they filled their cups and plates with our offering of wine, cheese, and sweets at three in the afternoon, the food elicited a few giggles and snickers. "How delightfully American!"

Apparently, despite the stereotype, the French almost never eat these things together. After years of study, I momentarily cringed at the thought this could be my undoing. How important could this catering part be?

During my defense, my director, Madame Piccione, noted the change of voice and tone in the fourth quarter of my thesis. She pointed out to the others that while it was a highly unusual approach, she had found it refreshing. She appreciated the odd sensibilities of her French-Canadian disciple. And I was awarded my Ph.D.

CHAPTER 14

A SHAMANIC
JOURNEY

———— • ————

The airplane door heaved open. As if it were the lung of a great living beast, the cabin excitedly exhaled its climate-controlled breath in favor of the rich tropical air. In rushed an exotic combination of fragrances, warmth, and humidity. It was as though we had landed on another planet, maybe even another realm. I gasped at the thickness of the air as I breathed deeply. It was our first moment on Kauai, and our only sensory experience of the island so far felt as though we were coming home.

Paul and I were blessed with the opportunity to slip away for a second honeymoon, and all roads seemed to be leading to this rainy little Hawaiian island. For years, I had been transfixed by the legend of Lemuria, a mythical lost continent that disappeared alongside Atlantis 10,000 years ago. Paul had discovered a few articles suggesting Kauai was the energetic epicenter of Lemuria, and that tiny thread was enough to draw us in. We planned a 10-day trip, intending to camp and explore the island in a rental car.

Before we left, Louise gave me the phone number of a friend of hers on the island, a woman who was a shaman and a teacher of Huna, the spiritual tradition of the ancient Hawaiians.

We were perpetually stunned by the energy and the beauty of this place. Most compelling of all, though, was a strange feeling of familiarity. On the third day of our trip, I called Louise's friend. Her name was Laura Kealoha Yardley. She was happy to hear from us and invited us to visit and receive a Huna session. We both said yes, even though we had no idea what that was!

When we arrived, the hugs Laura gave us were more like greeting an old friend you hadn't seen in a long time than meeting someone new. We were instantly comfortable as we sat down to talk. Laura told us about the island and its traditions, and about its ancient inhabitants who lived very close to the earth and were healers. She talked about a time when we were more etheric, more connected with the energy of the earth, of the stars, and of the planets. She mentioned that humans communicated with one another telepathically. This all reminded me of what I had read about Lemuria, and so I asked her if she considered Kauai to be the lost continent of Lemuria.

"It is Lemuria, dear," Laura replied. "The healing energies of Lemuria are here and the enlightened beings are still here too. This is where it all began."

The conversation continued for hours. Instead of trying to recall it, I think the best way to summarize what she said is to share a piece of Laura's own writing on the subject:

> The wisdom and knowledge of the Kahuna is very ancient, believed to have come directly from the ancient land of Lemuria, known as the Lost Continent of the

Pacific Ocean. It is also known as Mu, or the Mother-
land. The people of Lemuria were spiritual and mystical, and they realized that the one source of positive
knowledge was the Cosmic Mind. To gain knowledge,
they turned inward to connect with the Divine Cosmic
Mind through meditation and concentration. They had
great faith and trust in the Cosmic Mind, and in themselves as manifestations of the one Cosmic Mind. They
were able to directly tap into it as the source. They
developed the art of mental telepathy and were able
to sense other dimensions with great ease. In Lemuria
the teachings were pure, balanced, and honored God/
Goddess. The ancient mother goddess of Lemuria was
known as the beloved goddess Uli. She was the most
important deity in the ancient Hawaiian pantheon for
she was mother of all the gods and goddesses. Uli is
our Spiritual Heavenly Mother, the mother of us all,
the female force of creation. She is the mate of Keawe
who is our Spiritual Heavenly Father. Together they
create harmony and balance. Uli is the birther of self,
and by her example of self-creation she shows and
empowers us how to create ourselves exactly as we
desire. She is the female generative force of the sun, or
the Light of Life of the sun. . . . It was Uli who released
the Living Water that flowed in the Breath of Life from
Keawe. The Kahuna of Hawai'i were guardians of
this ancient lineage of the great goddess Uli, as well as
caretakers of the esoteric knowledge. For a long time
the carefully guarded secrets were in the hands of only
the most high priests and seers, and the knowledge of
Uli gradually went underground and the balance was
upset. Now, however, the energy of Uli is available to
all who call upon her. She is again coming forth to

facilitate the remembering of this ancient wisdom, and
to bestow her blessings on all those who turn to her.

Paul and I looked at each other with wide eyes, in complete
recognition of what Laura was saying. I had goose bumps all
over and took a long, deep, surrendering breath. I remembered
this way of being.

She gave each of us an energy session, which was something like a Reiki session, except with a noticeably different
energy. As she laid her hands on me, I felt wrapped in a soft
blanket of purple energy I could see in my mind's eye. This
energy was welcoming me back to myself, to my land, to my
soul. Laura said that parts of me had left the night of the car
accident because of the intensity of the trauma. But I was
safe now and it was time for the pieces to come back into my
being—the healer, the teacher of spirit. Gifts that had been
with me as a little girl but had been knocked out of me by life.

She also said Uli, the goddess of the ancient Hawaiians,
the Lemurians, wanted to work with me if I wanted to. Lastly
she said, "Anne, this is your path." It's been 10 years and I still
remember how these few words deeply resonated in me and
spoke true.

Paul and I both sobbed as we left the island at the end of
our trip. But we committed to come back again, and we did. In
fact, Laura became my mentor and kahuna as she taught me
about Lemurian Huna. I became skilled at recognizing different patterns of energies inside myself as well as energy patterns
in other people. I worked with the chakras—I learned how to
communicate with them and calibrate them within myself and
others. I was initiated into the Huna healing energy, which
manifested as a deep purple light to me, and I developed my
ability to offer energy sessions.

One day, while meditating with Laura in her living room,
I had an overwhelming realization that this energy I seemed to

be channeling was not separate from me. I had a strong sense that I *was* the healing purple energy. I wasn't simply a conduit for it by laying my hands on someone. I was it and it was me. And I could be it in everything I felt and thought, every word I spoke and every action I took. This healing energy was my life force, *the* life force. It was my soul, my connection to the Divine universe. I was the Divine self.

One night, not long after I returned from my last training session with Laura, Paul and I were at home watching a film together about someone's brush with death. The film inspired us as we'd both had near-death experiences (Paul's happened during a surfing excursion in a hurricane) and considered them among our greatest gifts. I wondered, *If I could overcome the fear of dying, could I do absolutely anything? How much does this fear hold me back in my life?* Intellectually, I knew I was eternal and immortal energy, but I wondered if perhaps I could release that fear on a deeper level.

That night, lying on my back in bed, I decided to meditate myself to sleep. I closed my eyes and began to breathe deeply as I brought my attention to my inner energetic being. I felt compelled to tend to each chakra with my breath, starting at the crown. I breathed into each chakra until I felt it energetically softening and opening up. I wasn't trying to make it open; all I had to do was stay present with it.

As I felt each chakra vibrate inside of me and open up, I gently brought my attention down to the next. The lower into the body I got, the more I felt the core of my body vibrating and expanding. The vibrations were getting slower and more muffled as I reached the lower chakras. When the opening of the root chakra happened, I experienced a high frequency of vibration that seemed to move all the way through my core, from the top of my head to the base of my spine. It quickly became uncomfortable and difficult for me to handle. It felt as though I was plugged into a high-voltage outlet and the energy was too intense. I struggled with the intensity, even rolling onto my stomach to find some relief. With my face in the pillow, my breathing became very deep and very slow. I could hear my heart beating, and it was slowing down as well. It felt as though my heart and my breath were simulating a death. That thought didn't frighten me as much as I would have expected. I let go. I felt safe.

Time stood still, and I don't know how much passed before I felt the need to turn on my back again. As I did, I opened my eyes and looked straight up toward the ceiling. To my surprise, the roof of my house had disappeared completely. Instead of a white ceiling, in front of me were green and purple celestial beings dancing among planets, stars, and galaxies.

What I saw was vast, without limits. It went as far as the eye could see and beyond. I wasn't just looking at this scenery. I was part of it. More than that, I was it. I had a sense of not being within the boundaries of my body anymore but unified with what I was witnessing. I felt I was back at the accident, experiencing an expanded awareness of who I was. Most of all, I felt loved, deeply loved. This experience was coming back to reassure me what I had experienced was more real than anything else.

A loud, harmonic ring resounded all around and through me. I was full of joy, and I said, "Thank you." Then to my right appeared a playful little being, a green light, inviting me to join and follow her. It was at that moment I worried if I went, I wouldn't come back. I thought, *I am not ready to leave my husband and my son.* Instantly, the vast space began to close in and the ceiling reappeared. The harmonic ringing stayed for a while but became fainter as the night went on.

This was a shamanic experience, an experience of the boundless and integrated Divine self as Divine love. It released my fear of death as it anchored deep in me a knowing that I was the entire energetic universe at play, simply moving through this soul, body, and mind—but not of it. I knew my eternity and immortality and that death was just a veil being lifted from our human perception.

The experience changed how I engaged the world. I became more fearless because I really had nothing to lose in daring to do what my soul truly desired. My life could be lived in service of this emotional and Divine human adventure and the untapped potential of the human heart.

I was passionate about everything I had learned about the inner workings of the body and soul, and I wanted to learn more. I began putting down ideas for this book, and I began to consciously practice living from a place of *Be* and *Feel*, infused by my soul and the universe. I was aware that the only thing that could get in the way was my tendency to fall back into *Think* and *Do*, thus forgetting my essential nature. It was up to me to stay awake to my being. It was my responsibility.

I felt I had figured out the secret to life. The more I became aware of the sensations of old information living in my body, the better I became at processing it as it came up. I felt increasingly lighter and more grounded. I could more easily discern the relationship between my thoughts and my emotions.

I became aware of other, more subtle sensations like the beating of my heart when I brought my attention to it. I noticed how different parts of my body experienced the flow of life force differently. Beauty in any form brought on a rush of awe and tears, and I could feel it in me like a rush of love. In all cases, I breathed deeply into the sensations, and the breath seemed to invite more movement, more opening.

I became adept at noticing the difference between energy and information that was rooted in the past and that which arose in the present moment. Present tense energy contains a peaceful sense of emergence that seems to be propelled by purposeful movement. Instead of coming from the desire to move after being stuck for many years, this movement and these sensations seemed to come from a place of life, a place of creation. The more I released my body from past energies and emotions, the more I became aware of this creative life force communicating with me through my body.

I began to live according to the realization that this awareness of energy in my body is actually my soul talking to me—it is a correspondence propelled by the life force within me. It is the same communication as the day my grandmother died, as the night in the car wreck, as when I stood in the classroom doorway on the first day of school. It is all the same, except now when I feel it, there is no need for dramatic happenings. It is simply there, without the dramas and the traumas. As it should be. And it has the same quality of freedom and excitement I felt as a kid, running free in nature with my friend. Life and spirit share the same qualities.

Although healing work and the avoidance of suffering for ourselves and others are important, they are only part of the equation. I needed to make my soul the leader, the guide of my life. I needed to make my soul my compass.

CHAPTER 15

AN AUTOPOETIC LIFE

———— • ————

I wanted to know now how all of this healing and transformation could translate into a way of life, 7 days a week, 365 days a year. Could my career really be an extension of my soul? Since the car accident, I had felt compelled to return to the inner peace I had visited that night. Both my healing and my shamanic experience had brought me to a place where I still didn't have all the answers, but my soul compass was absolutely guiding me. As I was beginning to decipher the language with which my soul was sharing its desires, I knew I would be making different kinds of life choices.

I wanted to know how this knowing could translate into making things happen, how *be* and *feel* could translate into *think* and *do*. I was good at making things happen before, but I had never really asked my soul what it wanted to accomplish in this life. It was more of an intellectual endeavor. In this new paradigm, the processes of desire and manifestation seemed to happen in tune with the way nature creates, and it looked nothing like the way a corporate executive might set and attain a goal. If I could identify my heart's and soul's desires, perhaps I could make them a reality!

In 2007, I had started a little gathering I called the Annual Autopoetic Ideas Festival. I'd wanted to surround myself with like-minded people and create a venue for people to exchange information and insights about living from an inspired place. I invited about 10 local experts in the fields of holistic health, arts, and consciousness to present talks on any subject that inspired them within these themes. The first event took place over the course of a weekend at a seaside inn, and about 50 people participated.

I completed the second annual festival just before I defended my thesis in December 2008. Then I wanted to make the event bigger, maybe even get it up to 75 people, and I wanted to include best-selling authors and thought leaders in the program. The desire was strong, but not at all rational, and I blush now at the list of people I invited to our little inn. I set about trying to reach the offices and agents of anyone and everyone who inspired me at the time: the Dalai Lama, Marianne Williamson, Byron Katie, Oprah, Matthieu Ricard, Wayne Dyer, Louise Hay. No one was safe from my calls! "Would President Clinton like to speak at my festival? We're expecting up to seventy-five people!" To my surprise, I received answers from many of them, and they all politely declined. All but one.

Deepak Chopra's agent was open to the idea.

The first time I spoke with Deepak's agent, I told her about my plans with the festival and she asked how many people routinely came. I wanted her to be impressed but not overwhelmed, so I inflated my numbers a bit.

"At least seventy!" I said.

She told me Deepak usually spoke for audiences of at least 1,000 and asked if I thought that would be possible.

I took a deep breath and said, "No problem." I still don't know where that conviction came from.

I needed to come up with the money to prepay all of the expenses: venues, advertising, speaking fees, and more! On paper this was probably a very bad idea. I was taking a huge financial risk on a venture unlike anything I had ever done before. My mind raced and played out various disaster scenarios. But deep inside it didn't feel like a risk at all. Somehow I knew, not with my intellect but with my inner being, that I had to pursue this project. I was making a decision that had already been made. I set about spreading the word that Deepak was coming to town, and as I did, it became clear to me that this was going to work.

There was only one little thing left to do: find the money! An interesting side effect of having so many degrees was that every time I graduated, I got a credit card in the mail. And I had kept all of them for a rainy day!

It was those credit cards that helped me bring Deepak Chopra to Halifax, Nova Scotia, for the first time in April 2009. A crowd of nearly 1,300 saw him speak, and to this day, people are still telling me the event helped change their lives. I was onto something. I had so much fun producing the event and now had a little business of my own.

After the event, a woman came over to congratulate me and asked, "What event management program did you take? Where did you learn how to be an event producer?" I didn't have an answer. I hadn't taken any courses. I didn't have the piece of paper that gave me the credentials to do this. For a brief moment, I had the thought, *Am I even allowed to do what I just did?*

Later that night, I thought about what the woman said to me. It was bothering me a little because I had always been a certification kind of person, looking for new titles to define me and show me where to go next. This experience with Deepak had been fun, easy, and successful. How could that be if I was not an "expert"? Suddenly, I remembered. I used to do this.

As a little girl, I would gather the kids in my neighborhood together and organize plays, concerts, and races. I would use the medals I'd won from my skiing competitions to give out to the winners of soapbox races. I would make paper tickets and programs for the variety shows and invite the neighborhood parents to attend. I can still see a large sign I made for a workshop that I offered to the younger kids in the neighborhood: ATELIER: CRÉATIVITÉ ET EXPRESSION (Workshop: Creativity and Expression).

The creation of the workshop sign wasn't my parents' idea—I truly wanted to get people together and entertain them. It also didn't feel like a choice. It was more like what Deepak calls "a spontaneous right action."

I'd forgotten about those years. They happened before high school, before I became self-conscious and began to try to be someone other than myself, when *think* and *do* got in the way of *be* and *feel*. Who I was, before I forgot, was a natural gatherer. I loved to inspire people, to entertain. Who I was, before the amnesia of social conditioning, was a natural leader. I loved to share, encourage, and support.

Deep within me, that was still all there. It had just been buried, covered up with layers of limiting beliefs and fears. The night of the Deepak event, I felt the joy and freedom of being a child and being guided by pure inner desire without inhibition. Filled with a sense of expansion and joy, I took deep breaths and heard my inner compass letting me know this feeling was who I was. I was this joy. It made me wonder: *What else have I forgotten about who I was?*

My business continued to evolve with me, and today it is a social enterprise called Autopoetic Ideas. Our mission is to amplify voices that inspire and to provide an antidote for isolation for light-workers through our gatherings as we help cocreate a better world. We have produced over 100 events and have created a boutique agency bringing support for thought leaders as well as emerging speakers.

I often share this story with friends and clients who are on the cusp of a major change in their career or business. I remember what it was like to be stuck and scared, and I know radical change almost always requires a tremendous leap of faith. We must all learn to trust the universe to take care of the details. Our soul compass often guides us into uncharted waters and to adventures that we never could have imagined. Whether or not a particular project succeeds or fails, I can honestly say I wouldn't have it any other way. Following my heart has opened more doors than I ever could have imagined.

That winter I had also fallen in love with the teachings of a man I had never heard of before. Through the beautiful words on the pages of *Change Your Thoughts—Change Your Life*, I discovered the heart of a soul who would come into my life and alter it forever.

CHAPTER 16

HEART-SHAPED COMPASS

———— • ————

If an autopoetic life had any rules at all, rule number one would be to follow your heart and enjoy the ride!

In the fall of 2009, Paul and I went to the Chopra Center in California to do a weeklong retreat. We both wanted to incorporate more meditation into our lives to deepen our relationship with our souls, and we were intrigued by the Vedic tradition and the secrets it held. That week was life-changing for both of us, and we came home with a daily meditation practice we still follow to this day.

At some point during the retreat, the facilitator asked versions of these questions:

What are your innate talents?

What do you really, really love to do, and when you do it, it brings you and others joy?

What is one thing that you do so naturally that you don't even think about?

What is one thing that you do that releases you from the bonds of time?

What is effortless and uplifting, something you could do all day?

I was racking my brain, but I couldn't think of a skill I had with these qualities. I knew I loved gathering people and it brought joy to me and to others. That met some of the criteria, but not all. I began to go down the rabbit hole of introspection, and suddenly, in my mind's eye, I saw myself sitting with my friend Rachel at a café. We often talk about matters of the soul and are always intrigued by what the other is doing to further her evolution. In those moments, I feel free from the boundaries of time and space. I never want the conversation to end—I truly am present and in joy, and I leave the conversation energized and happy.

That didn't seem quite right either, and I thought, *That can't possibly be a talent. It's just what friends do.* I dug deeper into the essence of that moment and what actually was happening. First of all, I was deeply listening, with intimacy and kindness. I was fully present to all she was saying with my mind, body, heart, and soul. I was tapped into the emotional and energetic content of what she was saying. My whole organism was engaged, feeling and calibrating the energetic content of our talk. Second, we were seeking meaning in the stories we shared, looking for clues, clarity, and perspective. We loved analyzing our stories and discovering new aspects of ourselves. Third, each could see mirrors in the narratives and patterns of the other. Through sharing from our hearts and souls, we gained perspective on our situations.

My own healing had changed the way I interacted with others. The intimacy and tenderness I felt toward myself manifested as a deep love and tenderness for others. I could be open and vulnerable without being weak, enabled by an unbreakable inner strength. I felt emotionally safe no matter what the conversation was, and I had come to trust myself and the universe. I wanted to share this experience with others. I wanted to be present with them in a way that invited them to safely explore their own being with intimacy and vulnerability. I deeply cared that the people I loved could experience this inner freedom. But more than that, I cared that as many people as possible could live like that.

Could deeply listening with tenderness and reflecting patterns with intimacy and vulnerability be a career? I suspected not.

On the last day, in her closing remarks, the facilitator said something like, "The information you have absorbed this week is all wonderful, but if you don't apply it to your life, it will just be knowledge stored in your brain. So, how will you apply what you've learned and make a change in your life? What is the single most important thing you can commit to right now that will change your life? What commitment can you make to yourself right now, where as you walk out that door tonight, you will begin to live like that?"

I felt anxious and a little uneasy. Up until this point, my academic and professional life had been about seeking, building, and then shedding identities. Would my quest for professorship be the next casualty of this process? If being a professor didn't meet the test of living 100 percent from my heart, would I be willing to write off the last 5 years of post-graduate studies and grunt work spent building that career?

I felt the pressure I was putting on myself to get it together and have my life figured out early. I did not like how that felt. But when the facilitator asked the question again, I noticed a strong pull into my heart. I took a few deep breaths and connected with the sensations in my heart.

My heart was speaking loudly now. It was telling me it was time for me to walk my talk. It was time to apply to my *every single moment* all that I had learned in the past years of healing. The single most important thing I could do to radically change my life was shift my inner compass once and for all: I needed to shift the seat of my identity and awareness from my mind to my heart for good. Not just the metaphorical heart, but the actual physical organ, the energetic blood-pumping and life-giving mass in the center of my chest. I could feel my heart so strongly—it felt raw and open, ready to enter a deeper relationship with me, a kinship of incredible tenderness and emotional intimacy. I knew if I could live and breathe with my awareness inside my heart, if I could be in that space, it would drastically change my life. Not just in the program room, but everywhere in my life.

I had a longing for my heart to lead 100 percent of the time. I was overwhelmed with exhilaration bubbling up from my solar plexus and filling me with desire, hope, and courage. Deep down, I knew my heart would not lead me astray. My heart was my soul compass.

I left the retreat center with my attention in my heart. I could feel the sensation of blood moving through and with every deep breath I took. I could feel the energy of the chakra as it delighted in this attention and communicated with me at rapid speed. I was saying a constant "Yes!" to my soul as it was moving through me, guiding me, expressing through me. I was in love with my life force and my soul and was ready to let them lead the way.

Soon after our retreat, our little family spent four months on Kauai. There I saw my kahuna for the last time.

"Now it's time to share what you know," Laura said to me when our time together came to an end. "You don't need more training or programs with me. Uli is working with you now. Just begin teaching." I didn't know where to start, and she said, "Just pick a date, send the invitation out, and they will come."

"Don't I need some sort of certification?" I asked.

"You don't need any more certification. Just teach what you know. You know more than you realize," she answered.

I committed to wake up with the sun and meditate every day on the nearby beach. With deep breathing, I communicated a great desire to my mind, body, soul, and universe every morning at sunrise for 40 days. I saw myself supporting others on their journey to an embodied spirituality and it filled my heart with joy. I was setting the intention for a life aligned with my soul. I planted the seeds of the work I wanted to do and I detached from how it would all unfold. Every morning I felt Uli's presence. I offered a *ha* breath in gratitude.

I scheduled my first workshop, and people came. I picked more dates and more people came. Eventually, participants wanted to connect after the programs and see me one-on-one—I invited them into my living room for tea and conversation. After a while, I rented an office space and made my practice official. People began to refer to me as their life coach. Although I never fully related to that title, I was now helping people come back home to their heart. It was truly an autopoetic process. I don't think my mind could have predicted any of the twists or turns, but my heart always knew. It remembered.

An auspicious meeting happened during those 40 days. For a year now, I had been in conversation with Maya Labos, Wayne Dyer's agent, to see if we could arrange a Canadian date on his next speaking tour. After many hours on the phone with her, Maya was ready to make it happen, but Wayne still needed to be convinced. He didn't know who I was. That winter, it just so happened that he was speaking in front of a crowd of ophthalmologists at the Westin on Kauai. Wayne suggested I come to see his presentation and meet with him so he could make my acquaintance and see if a collaboration was in the cards.

I was reading Wayne's *Inspiration* and learning how to plant the seeds of desire to manifest my soul's purpose when I received the invitation. At the conference, I sat in the back row and drank every single word this beautiful man was sharing. At the end of the show, I lined up to meet him. When it came to my turn, he gave me a great big hug and looked straight into my eyes and smiled as if he recognized me, even before I introduced myself. I'll never forget the feeling I had in that moment, like I was the most important person in the whole world. He gave this sort of unconditional attention to every single person in the line that day. I knew I had met a very special human being. Something was so familiar, and I couldn't wait to spend more time with this man. I told him about my desire to bring him to Canada. We exchanged a few words and I left.

A few months later, we were able to schedule our very first event together, in the small town of Vernon, British Columbia. Someone sent him photos from that event where you can see orbs floating all around him while he was onstage. It was such a privilege to get closer to this Divine being.

CHAPTER 17

THE END OF
THE WORLD

———— • ————

The Mayan calendar said the world would end on December 23, 2012. Much was made of this prediction in Hollywood and in spiritual circles. Doomsday experts had a banner year, and many people waited with bated breath as the fateful day approached.

We all know the world didn't end that year, but it was definitely the end of the world as I knew it. Life did shift. Old habits died. New ones were born. And I evolved into a new person.

I had started the year at a career crossroads, splitting my energy between Plan A and Plan B and finding the pace increasingly difficult to sustain.

In Plan B, I was a newly minted lecturer, juggling obligations at several universities while my children were in school. I enjoyed the connection I made with the students, but I was growing less passionate about the content I was teaching and that was proving to be a problem. In the absence of meaning and inspiration, work was taking its toll on me. I found myself battling with flus and colds more than I ever had in the past. I couldn't do it anymore. More accurately, I didn't want to do it anymore, and my body was telling me loud and clear.

In Plan A, I ran my own business. A few hours each week, I helped individuals on a one-on-one basis, and on evenings and weekends, I worked on my event production company. My business was growing, and so was my private practice, but it was never assured income. If I was ever tempted to completely switch to Plan A, my fears around money would stop me. I needed the financial stability offered by my university work.

Still, I wondered: *If I were to put all my attention and time on my passion and what I felt was my path, would the money grow and flow?* Would my lifestyle become like the one described in Anderson Cooper's essay "Why 'No Plan B' Is the Only Plan"?

I decided to take the leap and embraced Plan A. It had been a few years in the making and I was ready to jump, although I was scared. But the extra time in my schedule gave my body a chance to rest. I began to start every day with a green smoothie, which was full of organic leafy greens, and began a new yoga practice. A simple anti-inflammatory cleanse led to a radical lifestyle shift: I cut wheat out of my diet and gave up alcohol. I no longer wondered, *Is it too early in the day to switch from coffee to wine?*

I was delighted by the extra vitality I was experiencing. The colds and flus stopped. My mind became clear and sharp, and I felt more emotionally stable. Cravings for certain foods decreased, as did the last remnants of the feeling that I wasn't enough. If the body is the instrument of the soul, then I was feeling the effects of optimizing my instrument in the form of increased clarity and connection to my higher purpose, to my raison d'être.

By the time the world was scheduled to end, I had let go of all my teaching contracts, and my business and one-on-one practice were thriving. It was the year I jumped with both feet into my life.

CHAPTER 18

THE SPACE BETWEEN
TWO PEOPLE
IN A HUG

———— • ————

I t was the summer of 2013 in rural Quebec, and the battle-
ground was my son Olivier's eating preferences.

At home we were wheat free, and our children had
become more interested in food and how it could affect health
and well-being. While we didn't have wheat in the house, the
children were encouraged to make their own choices when they
were out in the world. Both of our kids had realized how they
didn't feel great when they ate wheat. On this particular day,
we were in a small restaurant with my mother and Olivier was
trying to order from a menu that was typical of rural French-
Canadian restaurants: an homage to bread and a virtual
minefield for a wheat-free eater. Adding to the complexity
of the situation was the fact that having spent much of his
young life hanging around Paul's restaurant, Olivier's tastes
and preferences came across as somewhat precocious. We were

quite used to this and were trying to make adjustments to some of the dishes, but it was clear we were an inconvenience to the chef. My mother intervened and insisted we make an exception and eat what was on offer.

Did she think I was inadequate as a mother? I was going to feed my family and empower them with the information they needed to be healthy, and heaven help the person who stood in my way. Then, at that critical moment before the fight I knew was coming, I noticed I was holding my breath.

I stopped talking. There was a bigger issue at play and it was mine, not hers. My breathing resumed, shallowly. I made a conscious decision to stay with the feeling inside of me and detach from the story. I asked her to give me a moment. I stayed seated and I began to breathe deeply. I let the breath run through my body, from my lower belly all the way up to the top of my head and then back through me.

Right away, tears began to stream down my cheeks. I continued to breathe deeply until I felt settled again. Within a minute, the intensity inside me was gone. I looked at my mother and smiled. She smiled back.

Then, very uncharacteristically, she asked permission to give me a hug. As she wrapped her arms around me, the tears came back. I began to sob. It was cathartic, as if years and years of emotional baggage were falling away with every exhalation. I sank deeper and deeper into her arms. I felt seen. I felt loved.

A few moments later, sitting across from me, she said, "You know, Anne, when you were a baby and little girl and you'd cry, I wouldn't hug you. I wouldn't come over to comfort you. It wasn't the way we were supposed to raise our children. We were told that it would make them spoiled, dependent, and hinder their ability to be autonomous and strong. But I feel differently today. I want to hug you from now on. Can I?"

I was awestruck by this revelation! I now understood where the pain in my head and the panic attacks came from and why I had cried so many tears in these past few years of healing work. I had been making up for a tremendous amount of lost time. I began to connect the dots and understood my awkward relationship with intimacy and vulnerability. I could see all the failed attempts at accepting love in my life, in friendships, and in romantic relationships. How many times had I moved away to avoid going deeper? I remembered the pillow wall I used to build between Paul and I in our bed so I could fall asleep, banishing him to the other side of the bed, protecting my personal space. I understood why my body felt such intense tension when my children expressed emotional distress and why I had to do so much emotional work to be able to give them all the physical affection my heart desired to give them.

My mother did not have the experience of a tender mother hugging her and neither did my grandmother. In one single moment, my mother had interrupted the ancestral pattern. It would not be passed on anymore. I remember feeling like I could now share anything with her. I felt a freedom, an opening up around my throat, around expressing who I am, and a new feeling of emotional safety in her presence.

If you think you are enlightened,
go and spend a week with your parents.

— RAM DASS

When I returned home from the trip and told the story where my mother and I exchanged that great hug to Paul, I was still feeling shaky, which was reflected in my voice. Deep inside my belly, I held the kinesthetic memory of being a child and wanting physical affection from my mother and not receiving it. This realization made me feel overwhelmed and ashamed. I

CHAPTER 19

A GIFT

———— • ————

In the winter of 2015, Hanalei began to experience night terrors. During the day, she was a joyful child, highly engaged and excited about life. But when night came, she was afraid of going to sleep as she anticipated another night of bad dreams. In the morning, she would recount stories of terrifying creatures trying to catch her and bad things happening to her family. As time went on, the dreams got worse and her nightmares turned into night terrors. They usually occurred one or two hours after she fell asleep. From our bedroom, we'd hear loud, panicked cries and rustling in her bed, then thumping on the floor. When we walked into her room, she'd be staring intensely at something in the distance and yelling in acute despair.

Often her gestures didn't look like her and her words were from a strange language. When her eyes caught ours, the panic would mix with relief and she'd frantically climb into our arms, like a scared creature climbing up a tree. She'd hold onto our necks and shoulders with a death grip. It often took a while before she knew who we were and where she was. She'd look into my eyes with the most terrified look I'd ever seen and she'd try to warn me of people getting me, trapping me, cutting my hands off, or taking me away from her. Her voice was different than her normal voice as she talked about our connection being severed.

The intensity of the emotions suggested a life-or-death situation. It was as if something was happening and resolving itself on a level I could not comprehend. I'd turn on the light, and when she'd realized I was safe and we were in her room, she'd put her head on my shoulder and cry for a few minutes before she'd fall back to sleep.

In the morning, she would remember the nightmares but never the terrors. We thought it was perhaps diet, imagination, or her unique vibrancy. From the time she was able to speak, she'd often express how afraid she was of losing me. It was more than typical worry about being separated from a parent. I often wondered if she was releasing past life traumatic memories, healing them in the night.

In June, I was in Maui taking part in a Hay House workshop called Writing from the Soul. Paul and the kids stayed home and I traveled there with a friend. I was back in the islands and feeling the flow. I was also feeling incredibly grateful to be a student again, even for a weekend. I listened keenly and took notes as I learned the ins and outs of publishing in the self-help genre from the experts: Wayne Dyer, Reid Tracy, Nancy Levin, and Doreen Virtue. At the end of the first day, I stood on the balcony of our room, looked out at the ocean, and expressed my tremendous gratitude for being in this experience, for being here, for being home, in this moment, surrounded by the beauty of Hawaii, filled with aloha and love. I thought about how far I'd come since the car accident, how my life had transformed so completely, how much freedom and love lived within my being now. I quietly offered my *ha* breath to Uli.

That night, at 12:15, I bolted upright from a deep sleep. A powerful energy had entered my body from the top of my head and ran through my entire body with such force that it jarred me out of my sleep and woke my friend in the bed next to mine. There was absolutely no content, no emotion, no distinctive quality to the energy. We quickly fell back asleep. When we woke up the next morning, she asked if I knew what that midnight event was about. I didn't but felt it would reveal itself as the weekend continued to unfold.

Later that afternoon, I was in the front row at the workshop, listening to Wayne tell a story from his new book, *Memories of Heaven*. The story was about a mother who, since the day she was born, sang a lullaby to her daughter that was just for her. When she was one, the daughter died and the mother was heartbroken and never sang that lullaby again. Several years later, she had another baby girl. One day, on her fourth birthday, the daughter began to hum this same lullaby. The mother froze and asked her daughter how she knew the song. The daughter answered, "Mommy, you used to sing it to me."

As I listened to him speak, I was surprised by the deep emotions that rose up in me. Tears began to flow, and I breathed deeply into the intensity. I was processing the emotions, but had no awareness of their subject. What a gift it is to know my body can heal so instantaneously, if I just let it and get out of the way! As my body settled, Hanalei came to my awareness, and more tears flowed. I realized Hanalei's fear of losing me was founded. She had indeed lost me once, in this lifetime.

After Paul and I reconnected in Nova Scotia in the summer of 2003, we both went back to disentangle our former lives and end our existing relationships. I had a friendship that had morphed into casual dating and anticipated an easy breakup. Paul's relationship was more serious and he wanted time to end things properly. In a matter of weeks, we would start our new lives together in Ontario.

However, life had one more assignment for us. I discovered I was pregnant and the baby was not Paul's. My heart was broken. I felt like life was punishing me for being too carefree, too optimistic, for daring to think I had figured it out. I was angry at myself and full of judgment. How could I be so careless?

I called Paul at 11 P.M. on a Thursday. It was the hardest phone call I ever had to make. He left immediately, driving through the night to be with me. It was a 10-hour drive, and somehow he found time to put together a care package. It was filled with food, books, and funny movies. When he arrived, we lay beside each other in my bed. We didn't say much. He placed his right hand on my belly, and I fell asleep for a couple of hours. He left shortly after I woke up, as he was due back in Nova Scotia on Saturday morning to cook dinner for a large wedding and didn't have a moment to spare.

The next days were among the most confusing of my life. I had never imagined becoming pregnant for the first time could feel so sad. I didn't know what to do or how to handle this situation. I felt trapped.

Days after Paul's visit, I went for a run. When I came back, I felt very ill, and later that day I miscarried. I cried for this life that had left me. I was relieved Paul and I could now plan on having children on our own terms, but I grieved the loss of my baby. That night, I dreamt of her. She was a tall, beautiful teenager with long, fiery hair. She was exuberant and she told me she would come back; she told me not to be sad.

That day in the writing workshop in Maui, I realized that baby was Hanalei. And I began weeping for my daughter who had to leave me once before. I felt like I had willed her to go and the guilt had lived inside me for 13 years.

I left the workshop room to get some air. I sat down on the beach beside another participant I didn't know. She was sitting quietly and seemed to be pondering as well. She asked me, out of the blue, if I had kids.

"Yes. Two. And they are amazing teachers to me," I said. I couldn't hold back tears. She took my hand, like a gentle shaman would. I looked into her tender eyes. I continued, "I can feel my daughter here with me right now. She is so amazing."

And at this moment, a little girl about Hanalei's age walked across the sand, wearing Hanalei's favorite zebra-print bathing suit. I gasped in surprise. I took a deep breath and one more wave showered over me as I released the last remnant of this guilt. Then it was peaceful. I looked out at the ocean in awe. We both sat in silence, simply there, present to the magic in the silent witnessing that unfolded.

I called Paul and told him what had happened. He wept and confided in me that he had been carrying his own guilt from that time. He, too, felt that he had willed her away. In the brief time he had driven up to meet with me that day, while I had been asleep, he had placed his hand on my belly and connected with a little white light inside. He talked to the little spirit and begged her, "Please, little spirit, I don't know if we are strong enough to raise you right now, I don't know if I am ready to take this on. Please come back another time, in the future, when we are better able to care for you, and we will be together then." He said he felt the light glow bright with understanding and then disappear. He also said from the moment that she was born, he knew that the little spirit had come back as Hanalei.

The next day, I got a call from Wayne. He told me he had good news. He said Hay House was going to publish my book. It was June 15, 14 years to the day after waking up in the hospital, confused about what I had experienced. I returned home to spend the summer finishing this book.

PART II

BE
FEEL
THINK
DO

LIVING
THE
SOUL

Dear Reader,

In the first part of this book I have shared my story with you. It's been incredibly therapeutic. Coming face-to-face with my own truth was one thing, but sharing it publicly is a whole other level of transformation. From the time I began writing to three years later, I didn't share it with anybody. Not even with Paul. It felt too raw, too revealing. Then I met my beautiful friend Renée, who is a professional editor and a gifted writer. I still remember the day when I handed over the first version of my manuscript. I held on to the pile of papers so tightly while she pried it from my hands. I was terrified.

Her feedback was the kind that only a committed friend would give: "There is a book in here, but this is not a book." For the next few years I received her gentle and clear feedback. She'd point out what flowed, what was compelling and powerful, and what felt contrived and lofty. My academic background made me write in a very specific, controlled, and measured way. It wasn't so fun to read.

More and more I began to trust my voice and the healing power of authentic storytelling. It didn't happen overnight. It took years of trusting the impulse in my heart and a deep desire to share. There were many revisions. Struggling with my own mind was hardest. Was this just a self-indulgent delusion or dream?

Is there a book in you? Is there a desire to share? I encourage you to share your soul story too. There is nothing more powerful than true stories of struggle and healing shared vulnerably and authentically.

Sometimes we need to keep these gems to ourselves because we haven't found a safe place for them to surface, or we don't feel safe enough within ourselves to deal with the repercussions of our sharing. But once ready, I believe that sharing publicly from an anchored place within greatly accelerates our evolution. We free ourselves from painful guilt, life-sucking shame, and all the other low-vibrational emotions that come with feeling judged by ourselves. Once that is out of us, we become fearless and unstoppable. We do a great service as we free others from the limiting belief that they are alone in their suffering, and we give them a silent permission to soften their own judgment about themselves and claim their own story, their truth. We become a good virus and a catalyst for transformation. It's through the power of narrative that we can show one another how we navigate this life and share the roots of our life's lessons and insights.

In this next part of the book, I want to take you on a deeper reflection and share the insights I have learned from my journey so far. These are lessons and tools I use in my retreats and workshops. I have taken hundreds of people through this process that I call *be feel think do*, and have consistently seen a radical shift in their lives. My hope is that it can be of service to you.

Love,
Anne

CHAPTER 20

FOUR SIMPLE WORDS

L et me now give you the full picture of the *be feel think do* progression, this transformative way of engaging life moment to moment from a deeper, more textured place within.

It begins with four simple words. Actually, it's four things we do every day:

Do Think Feel Be

You'll notice the *doing* comes first. Most of us are always busy with endless things to do and never enough time. We go about most of our days reacting out of habit, on autopilot, strategizing our next move, never stopping to ask ourselves why we do what we do. Often, we do things to keep from feeling the pervasive discomfort of just *being* in our skin. It's how we have been living for a while now.

We do so much, it's amazing we still have time to think. But *think*, we certainly do! A lot! Tens of thousands of thoughts a day, and most of them are recycled from the day before. From to-do lists to concerns to worries, our mind tends to chatter all day. It's exhausting!

As for *feel*, when we think about it, we don't do this one enough. We don't like to fully feel because we don't like to *feel* pain and suffering. Numbness is more comfortable. Unfortunately, the consequence of that numbness is it keeps us from feeling the peace and the joy that is available to us.

As we consider *be*, well, that is the big irony. We are human *beings* and we rarely get to *be* in the run of a day. Yet, simply *being* is the most powerful thing one can do to turn their life around. In the stillness, peace, and ease of simply *being*, we remember who we truly are. We live our life from our soul anchored in the body. I have found living from this place invites a delightful intimacy in our relationships with others and our self and brings miraculous healing and blessings.

Which brings me to the main insight I want to share with you. The four things we do every day—*do think feel be*—are at the core of our modern suffering simply because we do them in the wrong order and in less than ideal proportions.

For so long we have been taught to make our important decisions with our logical and rational minds, without taking into consideration the deeper, wiser, and more creative dimensions of our being. The invitation of this book is to consider flipping the order in which we engage our life on a moment-to-moment basis. I am proposing we reverse the order, start with *be*, and explore what happens.

Be Feel Think Do

I am proposing it is possible to live from our soul and to awake to the whole-body memory of who we truly are. It begins with noticing how your soul has been communicating with you.

Does this resonate with you? Is there a knowing inside of you that has always been there, perhaps in the background of your awareness, peering out once in a while, yet you ignore it the majority of the time? Is there a gut feeling, a twinge in your solar plexus, a stirring in your heart that lets you know something important wants your attention? How do you know? What does it feel like for you? How would you describe it?

I believe we all have it. I call it the soul compass because it is the bridge through which our soul and our "soul plan" communicate and guide us. Our soul compass is a Divine guidance system that communicates with us through the field of the inner energetic body. Although often more strongly through our heart, the soul compass can express through every cell of every organ and system in the body. It is an inner knowing that walks with us on our path and that keeps us attuned to our soul's deepest desires.

A compass helps us set our trajectory and stay on course when we navigate on the ocean or in the forest. We look at our compass often to make sure we are on the right path. In our life, our soul compass does the same thing. This compass resides in the inner field of the body. Every time we connect with it, it shows us where we are in relation to our soul's desires. It lets us know where we stand on the path and gently (or powerfully) nudges us in the direction of our plan.

If this is foreign to you or you are aware of this but haven't fully integrated it into your life, I want to help you get reacquainted with your soul compass.

Whether it feels like a fire, sounds like a whispering voice, or presents itself as a knowing in our heart, our soul compass communicates with us in ways that are unique to us individually. And when it does, there is a part of us that knows paying attention is important, crucial, and sometimes even a matter of life or death. Part of my soul plan was to become more familiar with how this soul compass operated and communicated. It took a lot of practice. The more we connect with it, listen to it, and act on what it tells us, the more the compass attunes itself and becomes a precision instrument. The inner field of the body then becomes a finely attuned device for the experience, expression, and manifestation of our soul.

CHAPTER 21

AN INSIDE JOB

———— • ————

G o anywhere in the world and ask people what they most want. The answer will most often be, "I want to be happy," or a variation of that. Happiness seems to be a universal desire. At the core of all women, men, and children, there is an innate desire to feel good, which has led humankind on a quest for more goodness. We have searched for it in many different ways, getting many different results. But the core of the search is the same: we want our needs to be met, we want feelings of joy and peace, and we want freedom from undesired feelings and experiences.

What I didn't know back in my early twenties was that true joy didn't depend on what I did, my level of material comfort, my assurance about my future career and relationship, or how I was perceived by others. I had it all wrong. I was letting the outside world tell me what was important, what mattered, and my emotional and spiritual well-being didn't seem to be relevant to that list.

If someone had told me there was another way, I don't think I would have listened to them. I had drunk the Kool-Aid.

I understood how to navigate in this material world and get to where I needed to be. And it had promised me happiness once I'd gotten there. However, that night in the car, I saw myself incredibly joyful and at peace. It was more of a felt sense than an intellectual understanding. I realized these feelings were who I was at my core, as opposed to something I was working toward. In fact, I didn't have to do anything. It was a state of being, like remembering something that had been there all along, but overshadowed.

Deepak Chopra says, "Be happy for no reason, like a child. If you are happy for a reason, you are in trouble, because that reason can be taken from you." This makes sense to me. If I am looking for a sustainable happiness that won't come and go with the seasons, then I need to be looking for something to anchor my happiness in, and my worth, for that matter, to connect to something that is everlasting, constant, and eternal. Something that is "for no reason."

If my sense of happiness is anchored in a pleasure brought on by an external factor, like people and their opinions, a lofty job title, or the latest fashion trend, then my happiness will be ephemeral and fleeting. It will come and go as people change their minds, material goods disintegrate, or status and success pass away. The same is true for food, sex, alcohol, drugs, entertainment, or sports. They bring pleasure to the senses in the moment, but are always fleeting and cannot be relied on as a dependable source of happiness.

For some, these fleeting experiences of bliss are enough to keep them going and invested in their lives. But for many of us, who hear and feel the call back to the soul, it's not enough to simply brush against the eternal; we desire to know it and experience it as ourselves. We desire remembering our essence as that. So we embark on the seeking journey back home.

I have come to learn there is nothing wrong with enjoying these lovely external pleasures. On the contrary, they are part of the exquisite and delightful human experience, but only as long as I don't look for myself in them and identify with them. If I want to connect with a deeper, more eternal peace, I need to place my attention and my sense of identity somewhere other than on the ephemeral.

The peace I felt the night of the car accident came from within me. It was emanating, like a beacon, from a place inside of my body. It wasn't an intellectual understanding. It wasn't conditional on anything outside of myself. It wasn't logical, nor did it come from common sense. It simply "was," without excuses, justifications, or explanations. It felt boundless and at the same time internally referenced, connected to a felt sense inside my inner being. Where in my body? What sense? It was difficult to say then. It still felt very abstract then, yet more real than anything else. I knew, though, it was unwavering, more grounded than anything I had ever known in this life. It could not be broken or taken away—all I could do to it was to forget to remember.

A couple of years ago, I came across an important social study on happiness, the longest longitudinal study conducted on happiness at the time, which illustrated my belief that true happiness comes from within. In 1939, researchers at Harvard Medical School recruited 268 men and set out to examine all aspects of their lives in search of the factors of an "optimum" or a happy life. It was called the Grant Study. For 75 years, the researchers gathered data about the men. They collected information about their mental and physical health, their careers, their enjoyment of their careers, the quality of their relationships, their marriages, their family lives, their eating habits, their hobbies, and more. In 2012, George E. Vaillant, who had directed the study for the last 30 years, published his research findings in the book *Triumphs of Experience*. I'll save you reading the book. After looking at all aspects of the men's lives, Vaillant concluded with two simple, yet telling, sentences: "Happiness is love. Full stop."

I love that!

Love is a big word. We all have different definitions and experiences of it. The word *love* can be used to describe the infatuation we have with someone or how we feel about home-made chocolate cake. It can be used to describe the feeling a mother has for her newborn child. It can define the message of Jesus and Mother Teresa's mission. In fact, it's a word that includes so much that the full meaning is sometimes obscured.

At the core of *love*'s definition, there is a common element. That commonality is the experience of connection. The nature and object of that connection defines what *love* means to us.

When this connection comes from our heart and flows through to the hearts of others and includes all of existence, love becomes more than just a feeling. It reveals itself as the most powerful force that exists and can be used to heal, transform, and create miracles.

Spiritual philosopher Peter Deunov (1864–1944) refers to this kind of love as Divine love. As opposed to human love, which can vary in intensity and come and go, Divine love is eternal and unconditional. In the months before he passed away, my dear friend Wayne Dyer spoke lovingly of Peter and this love. He would say this love has no opposites. I believe he was getting very close to this state with the foresight of his eminent transition, as it is clear now as we look back. When you were in the presence of Wayne, you caught a glimpse of this love. In that moment when he listened to you or spoke with you, you knew you were the most important person, that you mattered more than anything, that you were deeply loved. He was, and still is, a manifestation of Divine love.

Love—whether for a meal, a pet, a painting, a place, a person, or a god—always involves the experience of relating, having affinity, and being in rapport. And in relating, there is an experience of being at peace, because we know we are not alone, that we are sharing a unique experience of wholeness. It is the experience of entering into a relationship, connecting with and grounding our sense of self into something, somewhere, or someone. For example, if I feel love for my dog, there is a part of me that is identifying with him. I see myself in the sentient being he is, and in that moment, the recognition or reciprocity makes me feel "good."

So if happiness is love and love is the experience of connection, it makes me wonder: *Could there be a connection that has always been there—that has never been severed and never will? Could this point the way toward an unconditional and possibly sustainable experience of joy?*

The most important connection is the one we have with our deep inner self. The quality of this primary relationship will inform the quality of all other relationships in our lives. It will define our experience of happiness. Understanding, fostering, and nurturing this relationship is key to creating more joy, peace, and meaning.

CHAPTER 22

WE ARE ETERNAL

———— • ————

Perhaps you have had events in your life that have caused you to rethink who you perceive yourself to be. It doesn't have to be an accident. We don't need to wait for the dramas and traumas to activate our Divine spark within. It can be subtle. Have you ever had moments where you have known without a doubt there was something more than meets the eye? Have you ever had moments where you felt that a greater intelligence was at play and was requesting your attention?

Perhaps before you go to sleep at night, in between sleep and wakefulness, you catch a glimpse of what else is out there. When you walk in nature and the mystery of the forest overwhelms you with its beauty and wisdom, and synchronistic events abound. Or when you read a book that seems to have been written just for you and you can hear the call inside of something familiar and reassuring, yet indescribable and mysterious. In that moment, you pause and you wonder: What else is there?

The peak experiences I've had have taught me in such a tangible manner that I might not be who I used to consider myself to be, and might have missed a core component of this "life thing." I slowly realized I had been misinformed about who I was in a fundamental way.

We have indeed been misinformed. It's not the media, our teachers, or our parents' fault. It's no one's fault. As a group, we didn't know differently. But it is important to recognize we have been misinformed about the very nature of who we are.

I am human. I have a body that has been with me since the beginning of this life. I have an intellect that is sharp and bright, and I can freely choose with it. I have personality traits, I take on roles, and I *do* a lot of things. But what about before conception? Who was I then, before my mind, before my body, and before my personality and the things I do? What about when I die, who will I be then? Surely not my decaying body and mind, nor my ashes.

In reality, I am not my body, my intellect, my personality, nor the roles I take on or the things I do. I know this because in the absence of the awareness of all those things, in the car wreck, I felt myself to be far more than that. I experienced myself as more "me" and more in love and in joy than ever before. The same is true with my experience of my granny after she died. She no longer had a body, an intellect, or a personality, yet to me she was way more "her" than ever before.

Who am I, then? Who are we?

If our sense of happiness relies on the quality of the connection we have with our inner self, then who is the "who" that is "I," that is "you"? This is one of the most important questions we can ask ourselves at any point in our lives and continue to ask for as long as we live. Why? Because the answer is not the destination, it's an ongoing, never-ending journey through the great mystery. Our concept of Self has been so incredibly shaped by culture, religion, and the values of our family and community that much of what our self-concept is made up of is based on beliefs that are not true to us. Most often, our identity has been built on other people's beliefs we've adopted or past experiences we've had, which keep us much smaller than we really are.

We've adapted our identity to fit a world that mostly reflects a concept of human beings as separate entities from one another, flawed and fragile, always fighting against time and old age and fighting against one another to be right and validated. Had we known or been told at a young age that we were part of one Divine whole and interconnected, that we were brilliant beyond our imagination and loved and guided every step of the way, we would live in a very different world. I wouldn't be writing this book. We wouldn't need books to help us remember who we really are. But here we are! And in my mind, inquiring about this core belief of our identity is essential and crucial if we are looking to shift our reality.

Silently contemplating the question "Who Am I?" in an introspective manner on a daily basis opens our mind and body to what we have yet to discover about ourselves. And asking the question is way better than finding the answer. Considering the question "Who Am I?" without looking for the answer establishes a communication with the energy of the Divine, and little by little it expands our concept of self. It is like asking the Universe: Who or what is it possible for me to become, beyond what I already know about myself? It's allowing our own limitations to be expanded. Asking ourselves this core question also opens the energetic doorway to our soul compass, to our connection to *be*. We begin to establish a more direct conversation with our soul.

In recent years, this is who I have remembered myself to be. I call it my "I Am" manifesto:

I am not the body. I am not the mind. I Am a boundless energetic and spiritual being. I Am etheric and eternal, precise and latent energy flowing through a physical body, bubbling with possibilities and abundance. I Am one with an intelligence, a universal consciousness I call the Divine, and I share its all-encompassing, all-knowing, and ever-desiring-to-expand qualities. I Am this intelligence that gives life to everything. My true nature exists at a deeper level than what I can see, smell, touch, taste, and feel. Yet these senses allow me to experience and manifest in a concrete way my true nature in this world. Just as energy moves and transforms matter, my soul moves through my body and mind and transforms my being and my world. When the spirit that I am can't flow freely, I experience suffering. When the spirit that I am is allowed to move uninterrupted, I experience peace, love, and joy. But regardless of my experience, I Am Divine love and I am supported by this love, even when my mind forgets.

This means that at my core, my nature is eternal and immortal, as well as unaffected and unaltered by anything that can happen in my human life. My essence was there way before my birth and will continue way beyond the moment of my death. I have always *been* and my eternity is here to stay. And so is yours.

I didn't always know this. Far from it. And as you have likely noticed, most of the world does not live like this. Most of us were not exposed to this information growing up. Consequently, *do* and *think* tend to be our primary rules of engagement. *Feel* and *be* come as an afterthought, if we make time, and we often don't. By giving *do* and *think* a break and giving prominence to *feel* and *be*, we can bring into our daily lives our truth and really live it, not just talk about it or reflect on it.

CHAPTER 23

THE EXTERNALLY REFERENCED LIFE

———— • ————

G rowing up, I remember how important it was for the adults around me that I kept busy. If I appeared not to be doing anything, if I slept in too late or was sitting quietly not taking part in anything active, it seemed to bother them. If they noticed my stillness, I would often be asked to do something productive, to make myself useful. Stillness was uncomfortable and busyness was an addiction. *Doing* was an addiction.

I grew up to become uncomfortable with solitude and silence. As a teenager and a young adult, I became scared of being alone. I had this strong need to fill up the quiet and empty spaces in my life. I always needed distractions: people, food, alcohol, projects, challenges, dramas, new roles, new identities. It was uncomfortable for me to just stop and *be*.

My sense of love and worth was so tied to the external world's approval and recognition. *Thinking* of ways to be "seen" and "being good" were daily concerns from the age of eight on. Only later in my life was I able to have a full view of the extent of my beliefs around worth, love, and connection. They revealed themselves to me in multiple layers throughout the emotional self-work I did and continue to do. Every time a layer of shame or guilt is acknowledged, processed, and let go, I get a bigger view of who I really am and a deeper sense of my true identity.

Through it all, I've noticed I am not alone with this discomfort. In solitude and silence, unprocessed emotional baggage comes to the surface and can feel disruptive and intense, even scary. So we keep busy. We work a lot, we eat a lot, we exercise a lot, we watch TV a lot, until we are so exhausted that we fall asleep with the noise on.

It is interesting to notice what people say when you ask them how they are. Often, it is something along the lines of: "Oh, you know, keeping busy." In French, there is an expression, *pour passer le temps*, meaning "to pass the time." In the years before she died, I heard my granny say that phrase so many times, as if the point of her life was to keep busy, to keep finding things to *do* so that time could pass in a way that was comfortable. It's as if she was waiting for the end and distracting herself until then. The idea that time is something that needs our help to pass is a fairly absurd thing when you really think about it.

Unless we had role models who were highly self-aware and valued the creative potential of introspection and solitude, it's likely they, too, had trouble being alone, and also felt the need to fill up the empty space. It's not a judgment on them because they most likely had similar role models and were doing the best they could. But it is important to know this information because out of *their* discomfort, we learned that simply *being*—just *being* us—without any rhyme or reason, wasn't acceptable. It wasn't enough. We weren't enough. We also learned what we *did* and how we were perceived mattered more than who we *were*. We were acknowledged and seen when we did certain things that were favorable to the adults around us. Then we were a "good boy" or a "good girl." Then we mattered.

This is where the externally referenced life begins. The experience of not being seen, heard, or enough becomes too much for the child to handle emotionally because it is experienced as the absence of connection, recognition, and love. The alternative is to *do* what brings about acknowledgement, to unconsciously strategize for validation and attention. Love and worth become based on being recognized for what we *do* by the people who matter the most in our eyes. The way we received attention from adults shaped our definition of love. And often it was through means that were outside of ourselves.

Weeks after the car accident, I began to realize that I had to shed some light on the wounds I carried. It began with learning how to slow down my pace. Even though I knew a relationship with Paul would be wonderful, I also knew it really wasn't about him. It was about me and the relationship I had with myself. I remember feeling overwhelmed by the huge distance that existed between the peace I knew I could experience and how it actually felt when I tried to *stop* on my own. It was difficult, scary, and confusing. It was like I lived in two realities that were battling each other, constantly trying to prove the other right or wrong. It often hurt, literally, to slow down. It was frustrating to stop and feel anxious. It felt counterintuitive because when I did stop, I'd become sad and depressed. It just didn't seem "good" for me.

The next 10 years after the accident would be about bridging that gap and learning how to pause, interrupting *do* and *think* long enough to begin to allow sadness and other emotions in. My path was about *feeling* the emotional and physical discomfort of just *being*, quietly, silently, in my own skin, and really *feeling* what it meant to be a soul living in this body of mine. It would take 10 years to feel like I was living one unified reality in all aspects of my life.

CHAPTER 24

GIFT OF THE MORNING

————— • —————

What is the first thing we all do when we wake up in the morning? Stretch, make coffee, have a shower? Before that. What is the *very* first thing we *do* before we even get out of bed?

As soon as our awareness comes online in the morning, most of us put our minds back on our shoulders and we slip back into the suit of our life, the one we left by the side of the bed the night before. This happens quite automatically, and the next thing we know, we are the same person we were the day before.

Every single morning we wake up from the realm of the unconscious to enter the realm of conscious awareness. The day is brand-new and fresh with endless possibilities. Mystics and spiritual teachers through the ages have talked of how sacred and Divine the first few instants of the day are. In Hinduism, the time of day between 3:30 and 5:30 is called *Brahma muhurta*, which translates to "the time of God." In the yoga tradition, meditating right before dawn is said to bring deeper states of meditation, as the mind is effectively still from the night's sleep. Swami Satchidananda, in the *Yoga Sūtras of Patañjali*, qualifies *Brahma muhurta* as "a very sacred time to mediate."

Just as the sun rises, our awareness rises. Just as the light begins to animate all living things, our attention is bestowed on our body and mind, on our existence. Every single morning we awake from our rest to a day that has never existed before. A day with the latent possibility of anything and everything, like a blank canvas waiting to be painted. Every morning we have the opportunity to create a very different kind of day for ourselves; we have the chance to fill the cup of our mind and body with any thoughts, intentions, and feelings we choose.

We have this gift every single day . . . and we are also creatures of habit!

So, quite automatically, thoughts, intentions, to-do lists, and our mental and emotional states from the day before and our personality traits and roles relevant to what is currently going on in our lives come flowing in and fill up all that roomy space with mostly the same old stuff that was there before. We quickly establish the right things to *do* that day to support all the thoughts and goals.

Humans are said to have on average 65,000 thoughts a day. We know that our thoughts create our reality, so you'd think that with that many thoughts, we would have a good variety of new ideas and experiences every day. The bummer is that 90 percent of our daily thoughts are recycled from the day before. And at the crack of dawn, they all come pouring in, coloring the blank slate of our mind. If we are not aware of this, if we don't catch ourselves before it all happens, we pick up exactly where we left off the day before and not much changes from day to day. Our days end up looking a lot alike. The familiar days blend into weeks, months, then into years, without very many changes, and we wonder why our good intentions and our resolutions have not paid off.

We unconsciously jump back into yesterday's mind, largely due to the fact that our ability to *think* and *act* has been placed at the center of our existence. We have been taught *think* and *do* are directly related to who we are as a person, and that *think* and *do* need to take precedence over *feel* and *be*.

There is comfort in having our thoughts in order, feeling sure about what we know, knowing exactly where we are going, and there is comfort in keeping busy accordingly. There is comfort in knowing I have things to *do*, roles to play, that I am involved in this and that project, that I am needed. There is comfort in the stability of *knowing* because it appears to be the way other people live their lives and, after all, it is the way it was modeled to us our entire life.

There is comfort in *knowing* because in its absence we experience the discomfort of our body trying to get our attention, demanding us to *feel*. In silence, without any distractions, we often find varying degrees of pain. For some of us, it is a low-grade pervasive unease, like a nagging call to feeling something unpleasant, annoying. For others, it's louder than that. In the absence of the distractions of *think* and *do*, there is a screaming, a call for attention in the form of chronic pain or deep emotional distress.

Who we believe ourselves to be is often connected to the things we *think* and *do*. So when we interrupt the flow of our thoughts or take a break from *doing* our lives, we can feel lost. This is what happened when I moved to Ontario. My thoughts and strategies were life jackets, keeping me above the muddy waters of my fears and my pain. They kept me sane because they kept the discomfort at bay, when in fact, it's quite the opposite. They kept me away from diving deeper and truly meeting myself. They kept me away from unimagined creativity and a love like no other.

CHAPTER 25

SEATED WITHIN

T oday I can see that the constant noise on loop in my head kept me from getting to know myself and recognizing and accepting unconditional love. My logical mind ran the show and it was on all the time, chatting away incessantly, confidently in charge.

So where does this chatter come from? Growing up, the mind, which Carl Jung calls the ego, is conditioned to protect us from feeling too much emotional pain. And rightfully so. We need the protection because the environment isn't always emotionally safe. Our minds have the ability to operate separately from feelings so they can take over and protect us from experiencing too much distress. They take charge so we can become resilient to any kind of environment we are born into. It is an intelligent response, and we couldn't have done it any other way.

However, this process of protection does have repercussions. We were born with an innate sense of wholeness. We were born not needing emotional protection. But along the way, and to varying degrees depending on our environment, our sense of wholeness became fragmented. Our attention that was once on our entire being, and even included everything and everyone around us, moved away from that wholeness and moved out of the field of feelings within our inner body, and up to the mind and into the external world. Our awareness went from all-encompassing to selective and narrow.

Jung calls it ego differentiation. We adopted externally referenced beliefs and created externally referenced needs. As a result, in order to continue to "protect us," our mind is constantly controlling our awareness and "thinking" by trying to figure everything out while commenting on and judging everything.

As adults, we may realize our minds are busy and chatty, but we often don't know how to ease it. The protection from feeling the past hurt is so strong we don't know how to go about bringing in peace to the mind and the body.

When we were children, emotions were often considered in the way of our "common sense," and when feelings were expressed, they were perceived as moments of weakness or lack of control. Of course, this wasn't the experience for everyone. But I know it was the experience for many. And what I see today is an epidemic of individuals who have forgotten how to *feel*. Many of us have forgotten how to *feel* with the heart, as opposed to experiencing emotions solely in the mind.

Many of us were taught that in order to be successful, accepted, valued, seen, and loved, we needed to manage our emotions. That no matter what was going on, the emotional, passionate, trusting, and exuberant side of us, the one closely connected to our heart's desires, should be kept in check, lest more hurt would come. As a result, we end up as adults with lots of unprocessed emotional baggage.

Our chattering mind keeps us distracted from the baggage. The distraction of thought doesn't make the pain go away—it simply masks it for a while. It keeps us from feeling the pain a certain situation evokes, but what we often don't realize is it also keeps peace and joy at bay. In *The Drama of the Gifted Child*, a little book I highly recommend for individuals looking to explore the roots of their emotional pain, Alice Miller, a Swiss psychologist who specialized in parental emotional abuse, says, "It is precisely because a child's feelings are so strong that they cannot be repressed without serious consequences. The stronger a prisoner is, the thicker the prison walls have to be."

We can't be selective with feeling. Either we are open to feeling all of it or we are not. Either our heart is open to feeling the pain as well as the joy or it is closed to all feelings. So the journey is learning how to feel pain in a safe and integrated way without losing ourselves, so we can welcome the peace and joy and love available to us.

When we stop and attempt to simply *be* or *feel* for the first time in a long time, or maybe for the first time ever, it can be very difficult to trust that it is the right thing to do. It can feel overwhelming and counterintuitive. For some of us, the chatter in our mind is in place to protect us from exactly that so it doesn't let up easily. This is why many people quickly quit meditation after being unsuccessful at quieting the mind. I did that many, many times over the past 15 years. I'd try meditation and then give it up because it felt too uncomfortable and seemed counterproductive and useless. Once I began to do the deep emotional healing work, meditation became much easier.

A client of mine began drinking alcohol on a daily basis when he was 14, the year his parents divorced. Gradually, he became addicted to marijuana and then harder drugs. He came to me at the age of 33, having been sober for a couple of months, with debilitating anxiety and depression. He was overwhelmed by all aspects of his life and couldn't find anything that made him happy. The daily substance abuse had numbed not only the emotional distress he experienced as a child, but all other emotional experiences an adolescent and a young adult goes through, the "good" and the "bad." I'm sure you can imagine the intensity with which his body screamed when he stopped drinking after 19 years. He certainly felt the force of the emotions rushing in, but the walls of his prison were so thick from years and years of emotional avoidance that he didn't know where to start. So telling him to sit still and meditate would not have worked. It was too much for him to decipher and manage all on his own.

He wanted his life back, but he didn't know if he ever had it in the first place. The substance abuse kept everything "under control," and now that the distraction was gone, a freight train of emotions ploughed through his body, demanding to be felt when he hadn't developed any of the tools to do so. There was absolutely a way for him to return home to himself—with the right people around him, patience, and lots of love—but what I want to say here is that we don't need to wait until we are so numb to ask for help to begin the journey back home. We can begin to work with our noisy minds and find ways to bring peace within right now.

I really like Gabor Maté's work on the topic of addiction. Maté is a well-known Canadian physician specializing in developmental psychology, stress, and addiction, and his perspective on addiction really helped me understand our habitual tendency to run away from the pain our busy mind causes us. He says, "Not all addictions are rooted in abuse or trauma, but I do believe they can all be traced to painful experience. A hurt is at the center of all addictive behaviors."

I believe we all have, to varying degrees, addictive tendencies to distract us from that hurt, whatever it is. We all "use" something to numb the unprocessed emotional pain—what some call our ego or our shadow—whether it be socially accepted like the Internet, shopping, or workaholism, or socially frowned upon like hard drugs and alcohol. For me, it was alcohol, from a way-too-young age, but also creating drama in my relationships to feel relevant and validated, as well as keeping incredibly busy at controlling all aspects of my life perfectly. For my client, it was alcohol and drugs. For Dr. Maté, it was shopping for classical music. The addiction process is one we all share, it just varies with the degree of severity.

No matter how severe or benign, there comes a time when we are invited, nudged, pushed, or forced to look at the unresolved hurt that keeps us from completely experiencing the fullness of ourselves. Why? Because we are all human and we were all separated from our source when we went from the comfort of our mother's womb to the separated reality of humanity. We all share that experience and desire to become whole again.

Emotional traumas from the past that are left unprocessed increase this separation from our wholeness and the noise in our mind. If I believe myself to be all this intense mind chatter, I won't find a way out. To return to our wholeness, we first must understand a few things about how the mind works so we can help it quiet down and separate our sense of identity from it.

My ego is well trained. It will bring me around in circular reasoning, and I will lose myself again. However, if I can take a step back and look at my noisy thoughts with another lens, with the lens of a witness looking in from far away, I can get an unbiased look at what is actually happening in there.

At the beginning, I visualized myself as a tiny Me taking a seat in a chair at the back of my head, completely separated from what was happening inside my mind. This tiny awareness had no chatty mind, it simply observed the scene and noticed any thoughts, sensations, feelings, or images that may have arisen. Then I observed those thoughts, sensations, feelings, or images from the same detached perspective. This Me did not judge or try to understand, it simply noticed. From that place,

I felt I had more freedom to choose what I believed in and what I didn't, and what was relevant and served me and what didn't anymore. When I began doing this, I realized I had never considered myself to be anything else but my thoughts of how others perceived me.

In order to be able to extract that tiny person from the noise, I had to practice, practice, practice. I had to learn how to pause the noise long enough to create some space from it and then gain a sense of perspective on what was really happening in there. For me, this was the beginning of the journey back home, back to the other reality in the car accident.

Eventually, with the help of my teacher Louise LeBrun, I was able to bring this Me, this neutral awareness, down my spine and into the mysterious depths of my own being. What happened then was life altering.

CHAPTER 26

GATEWAY TO
THE SOUL

⸻ • ⸻

Health is not just the absence of pain, but the presence of an expanded perspective that includes the qualities of the soul. The processing of the old emotional baggage I carried cleared the pain in my sinuses and freed up the passage for my soul to express through me. I began to experience levels of inner peace I had never experienced before. I retrieved a joie de vivre and could see more clearly, like I'd moved up from my house in a small corner of a dark forest to the top of the mountain with a view of the entire landscape. This shift in perception was life altering for me. And the "connection to the body" was key.

The process of remembering the soul involves shifting our perception of ourselves from a finite individual, bound by human thoughts, perceptions, behaviors, and roles, to a creative, spiritual, and boundless being. Waking up to the soul is like suddenly realizing that you had been looking at your life through a dirty window without knowing there was a totally different view without any filters. It is a shift in the perception of our identity from the self-image projected outward to the Self residing inward. It can easily happen when we turn our gaze away from the incessant chatter of the mind and turn it within our body, toward our soul compass. It is the process of redirecting our attention, our inner eyes, to the creative and immortal life force that *unfolds and expresses within and through our biological body.*

It is a radical new way of living our lives, especially if we are used to knowing ourselves by our thoughts, our perceptions, the perceptions others have of us, and the things we do every day. It is a radical new way of living, especially if we've conceived of our body as flawed and broken, as the enemy that gets sick too often and needs to be managed. Our creative body is our ally. It just needs us to pay attention to its inner field with love, compassion, and patience, and allow it to do what it does best: process energy.

We are not our mind, nor are we our body. But the body *is* the gateway to fully knowing yourself as a spiritual being. That is why we are here. As souls in the spirit realms, we can't see, taste, hear, feel, or smell. We can't hug or kiss or gaze in amazement at the night sky. We are here to experience with our body the human life of a soul. And when I say body, I mean the emotions, feelings, and sensations that reside and move within us at a deeper level than the mind can comprehend. It's a *sensing* field, and we can be aware of it if we open ourselves to experiencing life more than with our mind.

The inner field of the body exists in close vicinity to our soul. The soul communicates through kinesthetic sensations and textured, intimate feelings in the body, and when we live with our attention mostly in our head, we can't become aware of this subtle communication. This kind of whole-body awareness is the gateway I speak about.

I am aware that paying attention to our inner energetic body can be a very abstract idea. We've heard spiritual teachers say it, but when it comes down to it, what does it really mean? How does one really go within? We hear the teachings say connect within, get in touch with your body, and nurture your temple. We tend to take it literally, and we feed the body healthy food, give it plenty of exercise, do yoga, drink a lot of water, and get a lot of rest.

Although taking care of our body in this way is very important, it is not what I mean when I talk about connecting with the inner body. Nor is it the awareness of the sensation of pain from a broken bone or indigestion. It's much subtler and it is present before the obvious pain arises. When our body is sick or gets hurt, we begin to play catch-up and we start to take care of it. But there is a way to be aware of our body's physical and emotional needs before it starts to yell at us in pain in the form of an inner body awareness. The inner body can tell us if something inside is out of balance way before it begins to scream at us with pain. It speaks softly at first, in the form of tingling, light pressure; a discomfort; or heat.

Before the full-body experience I had of releasing emotions, I wasn't fully aware of my inner body. I had glimpses that manifested in the form of a fire in my belly and a wild inner knowing, but I didn't fully understand that they were not only messages from my soul but were also calling me to a way of being and living moment to moment. After the first wave of emotions moved through my body in such a radical, new way, the fear of feeling that flow lessened. The first time, my resistance was so great it appeared scarier than it actually was. The times after that were easier because I had established a trust with my body and I also knew how free it felt on the other side. Now the resistance is rarely there and the wave feels less like a cold tsunami and more like the warm Hawaiian surf.

The inner body communicates with us what it needs to be both physically and emotionally healthy. It also communicates how it can be an ideal conduit for life and for our soul to move with ease through our body. But because it communicates much more subtly than the mind, we need to stop and bring some quiet to the mind so we can really hear the inner body's messages.

Making a conscious emotion–body connection brings us back to here, now, to *be*. It is taking responsibility for what lives in us, for what is our own emotional baggage. Making a conscious emotion–body connection is a bold step in the direction of making a conscious soul–body connection. When we feel emotions moving through us, we begin to feel the life force in a more sustainable way. The instrument of the body becomes tuned and attuned to the subtleties of energy and how it communicates. This process is like a muddy pond. When the dirt settles, it is easier to see clearly.

In this light, the *be feel think do* progression is a natural evolution that resonates with the natural world, and the way our bodies are designed. Accessing *be* through *feeling* the inner energetic body is the cornerstone of this progression. *Feeling* the inner body is the entry point into living an embodied spirituality and invites a beautiful coherence among our soul, our body, our emotions, our thoughts, our words, and our actions. When we engage our day-to-day in this manner, we tap into a flow of energy and the love that has always been there, but which we have resisted.

Imagine for a moment that your body is a prism, like the one on the album cover of Pink Floyd's *Dark Side of the Moon*. Imagine your soul is the white beam of light entering the prism. In order to express itself as a multidimensional rainbow, the beam of light needs the prism. Our soul needs our body. Without it, it can't fulfill its purpose. When the prism is clear, we experience flow and love and peace. When the prism is obstructed, there is resistance, and we experience discomfort and suffering.

Doing the emotional self-exploration work at an inner body level allows us to drop that resistance, to stop pushing back against life, and feel what is really there, here and now, moving through our body. We can then let the muddy waters settle and enter the current of life and affluence of spirit. Life becomes more effortless.

Living from a place of *feeling* and *being* is not always easy or obvious, but it is worth the time and effort. It's a brave journey as well as a sensual one. Every day, I am increasingly aware of how people are craving to *feel* more, to feel truly alive. If you have the right information and hold in your heart the desire to transform your life, you can do this work and empower yourself with self-reliant ways. You can become the one who cocreates your life with the universe.

Even if in the beginning the feelings that arise might be sadness and hurt, *feeling more* means that we can open ourselves to feeling more peace and more joy. Every time we process a repressed emotion we become lighter, our body becomes more etheric, and we become more soul-like. The invitation is to *feel* it all and use this body of ours for what it was made for—a vehicle for the soul to *feel* this human experience. When we can see our being as a processor of all our experience, including suffering, we suffer less.

There is an ancient Buddhist fable that illustrates the softening of our suffering when it is perceived through the expanded lens of the soul:

An aging master grew tired of his apprentice's complaints. One morning, he sent him to get some salt. When the apprentice returned, the master told him to mix a handful of salt in a glass of water and then drink it.

"How does it taste?" the master asked.

"Bitter," said the apprentice.

The master chuckled and asked the young man to take the same handful of salt and put it in the lake. The two walked in silence to the nearby lake, and once the apprentice swirled his handful of salt in the water, the old man said, "Now drink from the lake." As the water dripped down the young man's chin, the master asked, "How does it taste?"

"Fresh," remarked the apprentice.

"Do you taste the salt?" asked the master.

"No," said the young man.

At this, the master sat beside this serious young man and explained softly, "The pain of life is pure salt; no more, no less. The amount of pain in life remains exactly the same. However, the amount of bitterness we taste depends on the container we put the pain in. So when you are in pain, the only thing you can do is to enlarge your sense of things. Stop being a glass. Become a lake."

The suffering is not taken away. It is our relationship to it that changes. We are the lake. We are all the water in the universe. When we move through our world with a deep sense of connection within, we remember this truth in all the cells of our body. We see all sides of a situation and are not confined by the illusion of limitation.

CHAPTER 27

CREATIVE BODY

———— • ————

As human beings, we are not just static masses of flesh. We are energy in motion, and as such, innately creative. This is what I discovered firsthand in the Women in Leadership workshop, where I experienced the movement of energy rushing through my body like a wave shaping my being. I realized I was so much more than I had been made to believe I was. That day in the workshop I remembered something I used to know—how I had lived as a child.

Being creative is not something we achieve. Instead, it is who we are. We were mistakenly informed that creativity is restricted to art and a few special people with artistic talent when, in fact, creativity is the very nature of every single human being. It is the "what" in our biological makeup.

Newton's mechanical and deterministic perspective on everything, including human beings, didn't help our understanding of ourselves. This 18th-century science defined us as limited, flawed, and separate from the natural world. Although this perspective, along with contributions from many thought leaders, was useful and responsible for many mechanical and technological advancements, it was not an appropriate description of the human body or mind. This lens also had no space for any of the sacred or spiritual experiences. Nonetheless, we applied it to human beings and created institutions based on this understanding.

Organic living beings—the natural world and humans—are actually intrinsically dynamic and ever-unfolding progressions and flow. We are affected, influenced, and molded by energy in ongoing never-ending cycles. The wise texts of the Far East (like the Vedas) that were written over 3,000 years ago show that as a species, we once knew and lived knowing our creative and Divine truth, and we in the West gradually forgot it.

Now more and more of us are remembering that we humans are not mere objects within the creative universe, but that we are the very expression of it. As a collective group, we acknowledge our oneness with nature and are beginning to learn from processes we share with the blossoming rose, the emerging butterfly, and the cyclical movement of the ocean and the sun.

The best description of what happened to me in the Women in Leadership program is explained by epigenetics, which is a field of study on the frontier of biology. Epigenetics was born from research that proved cells respond to our environment more than they are controlled by fixed genes. This new biology demonstrated that our cells are dynamic and communicate back and forth with the different environments they are exposed to. The research also shows genes can turn on and off depending on their environment, including that of our inner field, like our thoughts, emotions, and beliefs.

This radical science, made accessible to the general public by researchers like the late neuroscientist Candace B. Pert and the cell biologist Bruce Lipton, tells us the human body is an ever-changing and ever-unfolding process made up of energy in motion that is interconnected with and responsive to its surroundings. The peer-reviewed findings tell us energy comes and goes through the field of our biological beings in a multi-way communication among our body, mind, and environment, affecting the cells of our entire being. This constant movement of energy means we are changing all the time. In fact, it is hard to resist this change. By virtue of being creative, change is the only thing about life that is constant.

When I was a teenager, I was told a very different story about the human body in school. As a result, I never knew I had a role in my physical well-being and that my body had its own adaptive and healing capacity.

But I did. My body was not stagnant. It was a creative process.

We humans have the gift of free will and we can choose what we focus our awareness on. We tend to place our focus on the things we can control and we forget that there is an intelligence at play in our life and in all life and that when we bring our focus to that intelligence, we need to *do* and *think* very little. We don't need to interfere as much with the creative process that is happening naturally. Actually, the less we meddle, the better. When a rose grows, it doesn't think about how it can grow faster or slower or perhaps become a violet or a fern so it can fit into a particular garden. It just *is* a rose, yet it blows us away. If it needs anything from us, it is love in the form of attention. With love, it is supported to become all it can be. The same goes for us. The same life force moves through us, and inviting and allowing it to move is the best way to let it do its magic.

Think about a pregnant woman—when a baby incubates in her belly, she doesn't need to think about how the nervous system wires itself or how to control the formation of the arms and legs. She takes care of her body and loves the baby within her, and loves herself.

The key element is the connection to the body. Often, when we talk about the body in a spiritual context, we don't consider its primary function as a biological instrument processing energy with every single cell. We don't consider the body as the primary gateway for the soul's expression. But it is where it all happens. All of it! So it's important to shift our understanding and awareness of its subtleties.

Many of us have read all the books out there. We know what spirituality looks like and sounds like. We are familiar with the ancient texts, with Sanskrit words and yoga poses. We can wrap our heads around the concept of soul and spiritual living. But what I am talking about here is different than intellectually understanding soul and spiritual living. I am talking about experiencing spirituality through the human body. I am talking about an embodied spirituality that brings us back home deep within.

CHAPTER 28

LANGUAGE
OF THE SOUL

———— • ————

D o you know you can tangibly feel an emotion with your inner energetic body? Do you know your soul can make itself known to you through the field of your sensing body? Would it be useful to have a kinesthetic point of reference in the body you could trust letting you know you are on the right path and guiding you toward your destiny?

The soul uses emotions to correspond with us. It's different than the stories in our minds about our emotions or our intellectual understanding of our feelings. It's about a sensation in the sensing field of the body, which is the root of emotions and understanding. Emotions are indications that energy wants to move and change is ahead. Emotions in the body are the bridge between the soul and our thoughts. They let us know the information we are presented with, whether it is someone talking, a song on the radio, or a memory, is important. Our emotions tell us we need to pay attention.

A perceived emotion can be subtle but often comes with a momentum and purposeful fire. If there is no emotional trigger attached to a perception, it is simply experienced as a thought or a simple experience of *being*, of peace and contentment. In those moments, we feel resourceful and grounded. On the other hand, when a perception has an emotional trigger attached to it, often because of past conditioning and hurt, or simply because of the beauty of the moment, the information is experienced as an emotion. When this happens, and especially if we are in public or with people we don't know well, we tend to not give ourselves the permission to simply *feel* this emotion. Instead we try to understand it, avoid it, manage it, or indulge it. But we rarely feel it in the tissue of our body.

We have been trained to rationalize this fire like we rationalize thoughts when, in fact, an emotion requires more than that. The best way to truly understand this language of the soul is through the subjective experience of *feeling* this force in the inner body. This force is present in all of us. The question is: Do we trust this force to guide us?

If the emotion is the map to the soul, the sensation of the emotion is the actual territory. Emotions originate in the tissue of the body and are experienced first and foremost as a sensation. Whatever we call it—sadness, anger, jealousy, resentment, happiness—the word we choose doesn't really matter. It's just a label, not the actual truth. If we simply try to understand and rationalize an emotion, we don't really get anywhere new. We can find a certain level of comprehension and it might create peace within us for a little while, but the change won't last. Using the mind to process emotions is not transformation. We stay in the map without getting into the actual territory. Therefore, we can't experience the richness of being fully alive.

Connecting with the subjective experience of the emotion within the body is a very different way of understanding ourselves. It's the experience of knowing our body as a vessel for the Divine expression of who we are. It's an authentic experience of life. It's an integrated way of being—mind, body, and soul.

In *Molecules of Emotions*, Candace B. Pert, who discovered the opiate receptor in the brain while she was a graduate student at Johns Hopkins University School of Medicine, talks about brain cell receptors. These neurons are responsible for the brain and the nervous system's ability to receive stimuli and create a response in the process of perception. Contrary to earlier scientific theories that only brain cells have the capacity to perceive information, Pert's findings show that every single cell in the body takes part in the phenomenon of communication. The entire body processes energy as information in a brainlike manner, and information-processing cells are present in all the cells of the entire body. All parts of the mind-body and all experiences are linked with the communication they share. She says: "What the mind is is the flow of information as it moves amongst the cells, organs, systems of the body. . . . Thus we might refer to the whole system as a psychosomatic information network, linking psyche, which comprises all that is of an ostensibly nonmaterial nature, such as mind, emotion and soul, to soma, which is the material world of molecules, cells, and organs."[3]

What this means is our entire being—our conscious mind, subconscious mind, soul, emotions, organs, feelings, and inner experiences—is essentially one large brain interconnected with all its parts. Our body is a network of creative energy in motion, constantly processing and communicating with its different parts, including the more intangible parts of the mind, emotions, and soul. Simply put, it means that by valuing the intellect so much for so long, we have been ignoring the most intelligent part of ourselves: our inner body.

Pert's findings were incorporated into many other researchers' findings in the later 20th century and have changed the field of psychology, validating more of the alternative medicines out there. We now know the mind and body are connected and that an emotion with its roots in the cells of the body has its own capacity to be processed. The mind tends to process information in a linear way with small, incremental changes. In contrast, the body processes in a holistic way, taking into consideration the biological and spiritual systems, producing big transformations with very little effort.

In fact, the body's primary function is to process energy very quickly and efficiently, transforming our biology so we can grow and evolve. Processing emotions at the cellular level creates deeper and more lasting healing than any of the traditional therapy models. And because it is propelled by the everlasting energy of our soul, it is a sustainable approach that deepens our spirituality. The more I allow my inner being to lead the way by fully feeling every moment, the more etheric and soul-like I become. For me, this is the path to soul realization.

If we can become aware of the root of emotions as a sensation in the inner body, we can go beyond the emotion and actually experience what the soul desires for us. When a soul communication arises in the form of an emotion, our job is to surrender our ego to our processing instrument—the body—by bringing our conscious *attention* to the sensation and allowing ourselves to fully feel the subjective experience of the emotion without judgment. When this healing happens through energy moving through the body, we can trust that on the other side of a deep breath, the soul will meet us. Expansion is always on the other side of this movement. Greater peace is always on the other side of the breath. Deeper intimacy with ourselves is always on the other side of this process. This is what fully feeling is.

We can trust it like we can trust life. This force shapes our body and life in ways we can't begin to imagine.

Come to the edge.
We might fall.
Come to the edge.
It's too high!
COME TO THE EDGE!
And they came,
And he pushed,
And they flew.

— CHRISTOPHER LOGUE

CHAPTER 29

THE ART OF BREATHING

———— • ————

For a few moments after the impact of the car wreck, I couldn't breathe. My lungs had partially collapsed, and I panicked. My liver was also bleeding. But in that moment, my body did an amazing thing: it went into protection mode to save my life. It tapped into its sympathetic system to stop me from bleeding to death, registering the message that it was not a safe place. If my breath was shallow before the accident, it got even shallower after, as my whole being adjusted to the fear. In the days that followed, the nurses in the hospital helped me restore my breath, asking me to breathe in as much air as I could and then exhale with force. But the full extent of my breath never fully came back until the day I truly brought my attention back to it.

If I had to choose one tool most useful for the path to soul realization, it would be mastering the breath. Breath is the most essential element for the survival of the human body. You can live for a long time without food and only a few days without water, but after a few minutes without oxygen, our bodies begin to shut down and our cells die. Breathing is the primary life-sustaining impulse of our human existence. Breath feeds the cells and stimulates blood flow through our veins, supporting our growth and helping us heal. When used consciously, breath contributes to the expansion of love throughout our body. If our body is the instrument for the soul, breath is the fuel that makes it work optimally.

Breath has been at the center of most spiritual and ancient wisdom traditions, with healers and spiritual teachers recognizing the breath as the animating principle of life. The ancient kahunas of Huna practiced the "ha" breath—the breath of life—to begin every meeting, every ceremony, every prayer, and every healing in order to support the manifestation of their desired outcome. They believed that when done purposefully, the breath was a source of mana, energy, and life force. They would sometimes breathe for hours at a time, bringing the required mana and focus to a project. The "ha" breath technique consists of breathing with a ratio of one to two: inhaling through the nose for four counts, reaching for the breath deep down in our belly, and exhaling through the mouth for eight counts, constricting the throat and controlling the air to make a "ha" sound, taking longer to exhale. It is said to bring into focus an intention and to support the manifestation of this intention.

The yoga tradition illustrates beautifully the role of the breath. For the yogi, breath is the tool with which the brain scans the entire body looking for areas of imbalance and blocked energy. On the in-breath, our awareness is brought to the fullness and feeling of life that pertains to our emotions and spirit. Stopping the breath short of a full inhale keeps us from fully feeling and from getting in touch with and experiencing our emotions. On the out-breath, our awareness is brought to our innate ability to let go and heal the lower vibration systems in our body. Not allowing the free flow of air out, consciously or not, and not allowing it to come to its full completion, interferes with our ability to let go. Without that full breath, we may remain unaware of the shadow, stagnant places inside of us, until the body and our environment give us louder and louder messages, sometimes in the form of pain or illness. Sometimes a simple deep, conscious breath is all that is needed for a pain to go away.

Breath has its own communication system. Consciously taking in and releasing air through our lungs communicates these messages to our body and our mind:

1. We exist here and now. Breath is an event that happens inside us, in the inner body, which operates in the present. Being consciously aware of the sensations and the sounds of the full breath takes our attention away from our stressful or limiting thoughts that are based on the past and the future and brings it back to the present moment, where possibilities live. Breath reestablishes this vital connection to the only moment that is truly ours—the present one.

2. We are safe. If our body can breathe deeply, it means it is tapping into its parasympathetic system, the growth mode of the body. In order to be in growth mode, the body needs to feel safe, as it can't grow and protect itself well at the same time. Breath restores safety and growth.

3. We are ready for change. As breath restores safety and growth in the body, it prepares it for the inevitable change that life consistently brings about. The breath allows us to open up to what is possible and connects us to the flow of change so we can navigate with more ease.

When we bring our conscious attention to our breath and invite it to expand and deepen, we create a life-giving environment within ourselves where growth can happen and where our perception of time can shift. We come back to the present moment because we temporarily bring our attention away from our thoughts, which bind us to the past and the future.

Most people I know crave more space and time in their lives. Breath is the metaphor for space and time. With deep conscious breath, we restore a balance of movement within our body, and this balance is reflected daily in our external experience of time and space. We slow time down and create more time for what we really want.

Even though we usually don't have to think about breathing because it kicks in automatically at the time of our birth and continues to unfold without our intervention, when we begin to pay attention to it, we realize we don't breathe as fully as our system intended. Without fail, in every workshop I lead, a few participants will tell me, "When you mentioned at the beginning that we were going to learn how to really breathe, I thought I already knew how. But now, I realize I really didn't." Every time.

During the program, I don't let up on the breath for the entire time. I myself breathe deeply as I talk and engage the group. My attention is anchored in the sensory field of my body and on the air moving in and out of my core. I am a hollow flute being played, without any interruption, creating a safe and sacred container. As people share their stories, I remind them of their breathing, and as people listen to others sharing, I remind them again of their breathing. I encourage them to uncross their arms, which interrupts the free flow of air. I invite them to reach for their inhalation deep within their belly, breathing in through the nose, expanding the diaphragm front and back, right and left, and up and down all at once, then the rib cage, bringing their shoulders back and down, taking in as much air as they can. On the exhalation, I invite them to drop their jaw and soften their tongue, letting the air flow out of their mouths, surrendering to the present moment. I bring them back to this breath repeatedly. Around day two, people come to me and say, "I had no idea!"

We might be aware of the benefits of breath, but the reality is that during the course of our days, we don't breathe optimally. For most of us, our unconscious breath is fairly shallow, higher up in the body, and we interrupt it often without realizing it.

This happens quite automatically when a stressful emotion surfaces. If it is sustained, it has an impact on our overall well-being and enjoyment of life. Our job is to retrain our body to breathe deeply and more slowly, especially in these moments of stress, when our instinctual reaction is to interrupt the breath. It will often feel counterintuitive to do so, even difficult, but we can trust our body's ability to process and support our health and well-being with breath.

Yoga teachers talk about it, Lamaze instructors advocate it, and even your psychologist might recommend it. But what I'm talking about is more radical than breathing deeply once in a while to help with particular situations. I'm not talking about breath as simply a way for supporting our healing either. What I am suggesting is deep conscious breathing while paying attention to the inner body as a way of living moment to moment, here, now, all the time.

We get used to our own range of breath, which has been shaped by our past and becomes shallower when the traumas are triggered. For a number of years after my car accident, the pressure around my solar plexus made me constantly feel on the edge of a panic attack. There was once a day, after having learned about the power of breath with Louise, where I decided I wanted to free myself from this sensation. I knew the feeling had to do with my injured liver so I lay on my sofa and consciously decided to show this organ some love. As I brought my attention to my liver, something I had never done or thought of doing before, I immediately felt it communicating with me. Just the act of turning my inner eye toward my liver was an act of love, and I sensed my body felt that. I could be the witnessing presence to its hurt.

At first, the discomfort increased. When I started to breathe into it more deeply, I felt the tightness in my abdomen also deepen. It felt like shackles all around my chest, iron braces guarding this pain. It felt completely counterintuitive, even scary, but I decided to continue to breathe deeply into that area. With every breath, I heard popping sounds and felt little bursts of release. On the last deep, deep breath, I experienced the space in and around my liver expanding as much as it could before it released what I can describe as a long exhalation—a sigh of relief that had been waiting to be freed. I became more grounded in my body and more aware of feelings in my lower body, like I had entered another dimension within myself. I was quite emotional for the rest of the day, having just uncovered stuck energy that had been imprisoned for years. I was incredibly grateful that I could heal myself in this way, doing my own healing work.

A few years ago, I had a client who was dealing with childhood trauma that happened within her family system, where it seemed to be affecting her current relationships. We had talked about her memories, and it was now time to see where the energy lived in her body. As she brought her attention to her inner body, she could feel energy moving in her body, but only up to her lower abdomen. The space in her second chakra was inaccessible. When she tried, it felt like a hollow, black hole. She couldn't feel any sensation. I asked my client if she could tell me where she felt the pressure in her body. Her eyes were closed and she was lying on her back. She said her lower back felt tight and had discomfort. I invited her to breathe deeply into the tightness to show compassion and tenderness to the area of the body holding on to something. Then I asked her to identify this tightness, to give it a color or a shape. It was black in her mind's eye. While reminding my client to not break from the deep, full-body breath, I asked her to gently invite the black to move from the back to the front of her belly. At first, there was resistance. She saw in her mind's eye a brick wall, impassable, with a dragon in front of it. These images were spontaneously being generated—she shared this with me while keeping her eyes closed. Although she initially thought the dragon was being protective, when she brought her attention to it more, she realized that it was her ally. She felt compelled to jump on his back, and with the next deep inhalation the two of them burst through the brick wall. What happened after was pure magic. Her entire being flooded with light and energy. Tears came rolling down as her second chakra awakened and revealed itself to her through a kinesthetic awareness. Her body trembled and shook for a couple of minutes. I continued to remind her to breathe deeply. She felt hot and cold. I could tell it was an intense experience for her, but she was overjoyed because she was feeling fully alive within herself for the first time in a long, long time.

Life hasn't been the same since for her. This "inviting and allowing" more *feel* and more *be* with *breath* has radically changed her conflictive relationships, but most importantly, aspects of her soul that had not been accessible to her before revealed themselves.

James Redfield once said, "Where attention goes, energy flows." When a nurse encourages her patients to breathe into the pain, she is essentially asking them to imagine the pain is breathing deeply in and out. The woman in labor uses this technique to help with the severity of contractions. The slowing down or the speeding up of the breath helps ease the pain. It communicates to the body that you are safe and supported.

Candace B. Pert relates it to the abundance of opiate receptors in the area of the brain responsible for pain control. She says:

> Conscious breathing . . . is extremely powerful. There is a wealth of data showing that changes in the rate and depth of breathing produce changes in the quantity and kind of peptides that are released from the brain stem. . . . By bringing this process into consciousness and doing something to alter it . . . you cause the peptides to diffuse rapidly throughout the cerebrospinal fluid, in an attempt to restore homeostasis, the body's feedback mechanism for restoring . . . balance. And since many of these peptides are endorphins, the body's natural opiates, as well as other kinds of pain-relieving substances, you soon achieve a diminution of your pain.[4]

She also explains how the respiratory system has its own endorphins to release when we bring our conscious attention to the breath and direct it purposefully. Dr. Pert was around when science was beginning to demonstrate what ancient wisdom has known for thousands of years. She was a pioneer in making this information accessible to the mainstream and giving humans back their power to heal themselves.

When we become aware of the full dimensions of our breath and we exaggerate it beyond its habitual range, we are alchemists. We can use the breath as an instrument of metamorphosis, manipulating elements, creating something new out of the old, and literally working miracles. The result? Nothing short of complete and utter transformation.

CHAPTER 30

THE TREE BENDS
TOWARD THE LIGHT

———— • ————

There are many modern self-help books outlining the power of intention in our quest for manifesting the life we want. But what I want to talk about here is the important tool we use in the process of planting the seed of an intention. It is our conscious *attention*. Whatever we put our attention on grows, so wherever we choose to direct that attention has a big impact.

Think of the soul as the sun and your being as a tree. For its nourishment and vitality, the tree naturally bends toward the light of the sun. We can do the same. By directing our attention toward our soul, by leaning our mind toward our inner energetic field, we increase our access to our life force. As a result of knowing this life force better, we can begin to align our intentions with the very qualities of this life force by intending more expansion, flow, harmony, coherence, and abundance.

Our attention, along with our ability to direct it purposefully, is the second most powerful tool we have, after breath, in remembering and expressing our essential nature as spiritual beings. Conscious attention is like a flashlight in a dark museum. Only what you shine your light on will be revealed. Eventually the beam of your flashlight can grow to include the entire museum. This is a tremendous power we possess.

The discovery of conscious attention is our key to a huge secret garden in our mind, which we get to choose when we explore. We begin to create space and freedom. We can take a step back and decide what we want and don't want to focus on. We get to choose instead of having our unconscious mind run the show.

I'd like for you to take some time right now to take notice. Close your eyes and become aware of your left hand. When I ask you to think about your left hand, what do you use to bring up the image? Start to notice and feel the blood rushing through your hand. Take your time. Be patient. Try to feel your heart beating in your hand.

What you used to make this happen is your attention. It is the same thing when we pick up a book to read—we use our attention to engage the process of reading the book. When we decide to take on a project, we use our attention to make that project the central focus of our life. When we express love to our children or show our affection for a loved one, we use our ability to lean our minds toward something in particular. That conscious leaning is conscious attention.

We use our attention all the time. Sometimes consciously but more often unconsciously. On the one hand, we unconsciously engage our attention toward things we don't need to question. For example, if a baby cries, we pick her up and soothe her. If the traffic light is yellow, we slow down. We brush our teeth while thinking about the day ahead, without missing a spot. We unconsciously bring our attention to a beautiful summer sunset that catches our eye or to a great tune we hum in our mind.

That's not where the problem lies. There are places where we focus our attention unconsciously and automatically that are not useful anymore. We don't pause often enough to ask ourselves if what we're focusing on is really what we want to be focusing on—if this person, situation, memory, emotion, or idea is adding to our lives or not.

We tend to keep our unconscious attention on things like negative mind chatter, unhealthy relationships, and traumatic memories. Or perhaps we keep our attention on the judgmental way our colleague spoke to us yesterday, on how fat we think we look, or on our ever-advancing age. Our attention is so often intertwined with our conditioned identity that we don't even know that we are giving it energy. This keeps our world very small because our reality becomes defined by these thoughts and distractions. It makes us more tired than we should be because when we direct our attention toward a life-sucking pattern, we ourselves become depleted.

The good news is we can absolutely change that, no matter what the situation is and what the focus is on. We always have the capacity to alter it with our conscious attention. Always. And when we interrupt our unconscious patterns, we quickly realize that so much of what we were focused on was no longer helpful and did not support our conscious intentions of creating more inner peace and joy in our lives. When we know that, we don't want to go back to the way things were.

If you find yourself spiraling out of control within your own mind, going down a path of *thought* you know is just going to bring you more frustration and suffering, STOP. Know that none of it is helping, none. Shift the focus from your thought to that removed space of the observer, and then bring your awareness to your breath. Don't let your thoughts distract you from noticing the sensations of the breath coming in and going out. You can also bring your attention to your hand instead of your breath. Breathe deeply, and focus on your hand and the sensations within it. Then think about an activity that brings you joy and go do that. *Do take the time to do what brings you joy.* The alternative of dwelling in your energy-sucking thoughts is not going to support you in any way, no matter how strongly your ego tells you it will. The feelings of joy, peace, equanimity, love, and emotional nourishment will support you; you just have to trust that and trust yourself.

Becoming familiar with our attention and observing how it habitually works and how we can direct it consciously empowers us. It helps us become active players in our lives. It puts us in the driver's seat.

We can use our conscious attention when we feel overwhelmed, stressed, or not resourceful, or when we have some time to relax and rest into our own being. Practicing conscious attention in moments of calm can give us the experience we need for those moments when it is harder to detach ourselves from the situation and become the observer.

Choosing to place our attention within helps us focus on who we really are and not on what we have been made to believe we are or what we should be. With our attention, we can choose to take energy away from the conditioned self and the mind chatter—this will keep us in *thinking* and *doing* mode, and allow silence, peace, and space to *be* "now" in our being.

That quiet and peaceful space of *be* is where our soul corresponds with us. It is our soul compass and a place we can live from. It is where we can experience the expanded dimension of who we really are. It is the sacred silence, the gateway to deeper levels of awareness. And the beauty of it is that it has been and will always be there. It is the sun behind the clouds, shining bright and full of wisdom, vitality, and unconditional love, even if we can't see it. Our soul will always be there, patiently waiting for our gaze, our *attention*, no matter how long we have been looking away. It will always desire to guide us.

CHAPTER 31

HEART THE
NEW BRAIN

———— • ————

L ooking back, I see the day in the program room at the Chopra Center as the day of the Great Meeting. It was the day where, after years of letting down my guard and softening my edges, I was ready to be in the presence of my heart and truly able to accept such a love to guide me. It was echoing the love I felt after my grandmother died, the love Paul shared with me, the love I felt in the presence of the parallel life I experienced the night of the car accident, the love I saw in Olivier's eyes, and the love of life Hanalei exuberantly demonstrated every second of every day.

As it turned out, I was this love. It had been mirroring itself to me so I could remember who I truly was. I was now the one offering it to myself, willingly. This unconditional and Divine love was not just an external force I accepted in my life as a catalyst for healing and growth; it was also a great internal force from which I wasn't separate. This inner force desired to express itself in the world more than anything.

My new relationship with my heart was complex, yet simple at the same time. I now understood that I had tapped into an infinite well of possibilities. My heart held tremendous courage and intelligence, and I couldn't possibly understand its full depth. But I didn't have to completely understand what was working under the surface. I could trust and surrender to it. Its own innate mechanism operated at a greater speed and efficiency than any processes or strategies I had used before. All I had to *do* was trust and get out of the way.

The heart had me enthralled, and the subsequent research I did fascinated me. I discovered the HeartMath Institute, an organization based out of California whose mission is to help bring mind-body emotion into balanced alignment with the heart's wisdom. They contend the heart is the master organ of the body and its ability to process knowledge is greater than any other organ, including the brain. Rollin McCraty, Ph.D., vice president and director of research at the institute, explains, "The heart generates the largest electromagnetic field in the body. The electrical field . . . is about 60 times greater in amplitude than the brain waves. . . . The magnetic component of the heart's field, which is around 100 times stronger than that produced by the brain . . . can be measured several feet away from the body." To me, this indicates why it can sometimes be an overwhelming feeling to connect with the heart and why we are often afraid of trusting our hearts. It is because the life force is so powerful.

I also discovered that the heart possesses 40,000 sensory neurites, which means the heart communicates with the brain and the rest of the body and affects our emotional, physiological, and spiritual health in a similar way to our brain. However, the heart can sense, feel, and know at a greater speed than the brain.

Emotions have an important impact on the heart's health. As we have seen in previous chapters, the emotions and organs in the body are interconnected through cell communication. It is said that emotions of fear and protection interfere with the optimal health of the heart by disrupting the innate coherent rhythm it needs for optimal functioning as a life-sustaining organ. On the other hand, emotions of love, peace, equanimity, and love harmonize the heart's rhythm and restore balance in the nervous system, bringing well-being to the body. When the heart and the body are well, the mind follows.

Most intriguing to me is HeartMath's research into the uncovering of intelligence when attention is consciously directed toward the organ of the heart, causing expansive emotions to be induced or experienced in the heart space. McCraty says:

> The intuitive heart is what people have associated with their "inner voice" throughout history. Each year, more and more people are including the practice of "listening" to their hearts for inner guidance or to what some refer to as their "higher power"—a source of wisdom and intelligence. In research conducted in our laboratory, we found that coherence is of prime importance in connecting us with our intuitive inner guidance. There is compelling evidence to suggest that the heart's energy field (energetic heart) is coupled to a field of information that is not bound by the classic limits of time and space. This evidence comes from a rigorous experimental study that investigated the proposition that the body receives and processes information about a future event before the event actually happens. The study's results provide surprising data showing that both the heart and brain receive and respond to pre-stimulus information about a future event. Even more tantalizing are indications that the heart receives intuitive information before the brain does.[5]

This corroborates with my experiences during both healings and peak experiences in my life. It confirms that my heart and the cells in my body *know* information before my intellect does. And this information, which I absorb as a sensory experience, is a communication from my own intuitive guidance system. The more I express my emotions, the more I allow the movement of energy to move through the cells of my body with breath. The more I heal my heart, the more I can access and live from my soul.

Now I see thinking in this manner as a whole-body process of the soul more than a process of the intellectual mind. Thoughts have become a by-product of a soul-heart-body-mind correspondence, in that order. In *Hua Hu Ching: The Unknown Teachings of Lao Tzu*, Brian Walker translated the 35th teaching like this:

> Intellectual knowledge exists in and of the brain.
> Because the brain is part of the body, which must one day expire, this collection of facts, however large and impressive, will expire as well.
> Insight, however, is a function of the spirit.
> Because your spirit follows you through cycle after cycle of life, death, and rebirth, you have the opportunity of cultivating insight in an ongoing fashion.
> Refined over time, insight becomes pure, constant, and unwavering.
> This is the beginning of immortality.

Insights are like revelations that arise from within, and when the intellect becomes aware of them, perception is expanded and our perception of reality shifts. Insights have a lasting and anchored quality to them. They make us feel grounded in what we know, more than if we were to understand solely with our intellect. It's whole-being knowing. In the *be feel think do* progression, insights come from the soul and guide our actions, our projects, and the things we say and do.

The more I live from my heart, the more I notice insights appearing spontaneously and effortlessly in my awareness. The insights come to me through dreams, intuition, gut feeling, images, sounds, colors, or simply a deep knowing within my heart.

Living with my attention in my heart has become a way of *being* day to day, moment to moment, breath to breath. There is a force within my heart that has desires and wants to *do* certain things. The more I trust what my heart and my body communicate, the less dissonance I have between what I *feel* inside and what I say and *do* on the outside.

My inner and outer worlds have merged into one. That's true freedom!

CHAPTER 32

FIRST CHOICE,
LAST FREEDOM

———— • ————

I 'll tell you why today I consider my mother to be my great-est teacher.

      In my early twenties, when I'd go visit my mother, there was very little space between her saying something to me, me feeling judged, and us arguing. I'd go from calm to see-ing red in an instant. She'd say something benign like, "It looks like you have dyed your hair. Oh, I miss your natural hair," or, "You look tired. You gained weight." And I would think to myself, *Of course, there she goes criticizing me yet again. I'm never good enough for her.* And the resentment stayed within me and set the tone for the day or sometimes the entire visit.

      In a way, I was setting it up. I was expecting her to say something I didn't like. Unconsciously, I really was waiting for it to happen so I could be justified in how unloved I felt. This was my petty inner dialogue. I was making a reality out of what was going on in my own mind. It didn't matter if her intentions were good or not. Once I arrived, before we even exchanged a word, the pattern was already engaged, and she didn't stand a chance. As years went by, we were both aware our interactions were not healthy or pleasant, yet neither of us seemed to know how to change things. We even wondered if we would be able to continue having a relationship.

After the imaginary conversation with her in the cottage, things did change a lot. What happened that day was I had given myself the permission to love myself, to attend and tend to the child in me that was holding unresolved hurt. And by extending that act of love and compassion toward myself first, I had an increased capacity to extend acts of love and compassion toward others, in this case, my mother. It was much easier for me to see how we could understand each other and begin to connect more.

The healing created more space in my being, softening my heart and allowing me to see that I ultimately had the freedom to decide. In the heat of the moment of an argument, there was a choice point. Before the thoughts of blame would run through my head and the angry words out of my mouth, there was a feeling of hurt within me, a sadness. Before, there was no awareness of any feelings of any kind, except indignation, which pushed me to react toward her. After the healing happened, I completely stopped projecting that hurt onto her. I was able to observe and own the hurt that was mine. I was able to consider the idea she wasn't saying anything to be hurtful. It was her way of showing me her love in the only way she knew how.

The next time I saw my mother, a wonderful thing happened. In a moment of hurt, I felt tremendous compassion between our hearts. There was compassion for the little girl in me who felt unseen and needed tenderness. There was compassion for my mother, who was going through the experience, over and over again, every time I got upset, of feeling like an inadequate mother. Compassion for the understanding and tenderness she never received from her own parents. It was all so clear. All these feelings could coexist in that moment. One didn't make the other not true.

With that perspective came a very important *choice*. In moments of intensity, I could now choose to extend that gesture of compassion, to myself first by breathing deeply and bringing my attention to the impulse in me, and then to the person in front of me by listening with more compassionate ears. That was my choice to make, my freedom to take. Not the person in front of me's choice, not my mother's, but my own. That moment of realization was so empowering. I could no longer be the victim of others' behaviors. I was ultimately free.

When we become aware of the unconscious choices we make, we can decide to change them. Viktor Frankl (1905–1997), who was a brilliant psychiatrist as well as a Holocaust survivor, reminds us of that choice. In Frankl's book *Man's Search for Meaning* (1946), which sold over 10 million copies by the time of his death in 1997, he explains how the prisoners' ability to choose what they focused on and believed in— especially if they were able to imagine a positive future in the face of their bleak and seemingly hopeless situation—greatly affected their longevity. He asks the reader to ponder how much power we actually have in the face of the worst situation:

> Do the prisoners' reactions to the singular world of the concentration camp prove that man cannot escape the influences of his surroundings? Does man have no choice of action in the face of such circumstances? We can answer these questions from experience as well as on principle. The experiences of camp life show that man does have a choice of action. There were enough examples, often of a heroic nature, which proved that apathy could be overcome, irritability suppressed. Man can preserve a vestige of spiritual freedom, of

independence of mind, even in such terrible conditions of psychic and physical stress. We who lived in concentration camps can remember the men who walked through the huts comforting others, giving away their last piece of bread. They may have been few in number, but they offer sufficient proof that everything can be taken from a man but one thing: the last of the human freedoms—to choose one's attitude in any given set of circumstances, to choose one's own way.[6]

When I really began to think about these men and women in the camps and how their ability to choose their state of being was their last freedom, and how when they chose love and compassion they had a very different experience, something in me clicked like never before. That was the day I stopped blaming others and circumstances for my unhappiness. That was the day when I realized that I was the one responsible for my own happiness. I had been redirecting my energy, taking it outward and back into myself. I had been wasting energy blaming others. No matter what had happened to me in the past, I alone was the one who had to do the work to heal. And no matter what had happened to me in my childhood, how I chose to be and feel in the current moment had the power to set me free from all of it.

Choosing love and compassion is always the best choice. And no one can remind me of this as much as my mother does. In her presence, I am invited more than ever to go deeper into this love and compassion. She is the Divine invitation, and I choose to accept it.

Frankl's experience and wisdom remind us of the freedom we have each and every moment in choosing our destiny. And it starts with the simple choice of the attitude we have in the face of adversity, big or small. If men and women in concentration camps with no physical freedom were still able to find love and meaning within their hearts, choosing our attitude in the face of adversity is a possible endeavor for every one of us, at any time.

Every single moment of our existence, every time the "now" comes around, whether we are in a place where we perceive ourselves to be free or not, we always have the freedom to choose where we place our attention. That is a great gift, one we've always had and will always have. Even not choosing is a choice. Yet we forget this freedom easily. Years and years of holding on to a limited identity of someone at the mercy of factors out of our control makes it difficult for us to see the space available for us to make a different choice.

The late Dr. David Simon, co-founder of the Chopra Center, said in his book *Free to Love, Free to Heal*, "The essence of responsibility is recognizing that regardless of what has happened up until now, we are capable of making new choices that can improve our situation moving forward. We always have the ability to respond in creative ways that allow for something new to emerge."[7] When we realize that we have this freedom of choice, we get to insert space in the continual flow of thought, where there was no space previously. We shine the light of awareness where there was no light.

In doubt, I always bring my attention to my heart. If I am lost, confused, overwhelmed, or have forgotten how to find my grounding, I bring my attention to my heart, breathe deeply, and invite in a loving feeling. But I have to choose this. It's not always easy because often the desire to be right is stronger than the desire for peace. But I have experienced it enough times now to know that justification never leads to a good place. Love does. Always.

We get to decide the experiences we want and the ones we want to change. We choose where the line in the sand is drawn, and when we say yes and when we say no. We get to choose the company we keep and the attitude we have with the company we didn't get to choose. When we unconsciously gravitate toward certain kinds of people, we can ask ourselves if these relationships still serve us and add to the love ratio in our life or if we tend to keep ourselves small and tight when in this company.

We get to choose the kinds of conversations we have and the kind of information we listen to. Does turning on the news or checking your e-mails first thing in the morning make you feel stressed or upset and set the tone for the day? Does talking to certain people give you a recurring feeling of emptiness and disappointment in yourself? In all situations, we can ask ourselves: Do I feel my being expanding or contracting right now? Is love, abundance, and gratitude present or is it fear, lack, and resentment?

Just the simple choice to direct our attention away from where we normally unconsciously have our attention is a powerful decision. It tells the body and mind that we desire something new and are not interested in letting recycled information guide the way. It is a conscious movement toward *be*.

The same goes for leaning our attention toward something we consciously desire. If we consciously desire more space and inner peace, choosing to lean our attention many times a day toward a deep full-body breath and awareness of the body's inner energetic field will increase that state of inner peace. If we consciously desire more expression and experiences of joy and love, choosing to lean our attention toward our heart center, to feel and extend that love and joy toward another person, will encourage our body to feel those feelings more often and energetically attract experiences that will make us feel these feelings. It tells our body that this state is important and that these feelings are a priority.

We can also choose to have a more compassionate dialogue within ourselves that is kind, accepting, and loving. We can choose to talk to ourselves the way we talk to someone we care about. When I became aware of my inner dialogue for the first time, I was surprised that no one in my life spoke to me as harshly as I did. It was quite the revelation. Notice what tone you use when you communicate in your own mind. Are you judgmental or understanding? Are you hard on yourself or kind and gentle? Our inner dialogue greatly affects our reality, so shifting its quality will support the changes we want within and without.

We all have different beliefs about where we came from and where we were before we were born, and the belief we hold about our origin can influence how we live our lives.

At this point in my life, I feel strongly I exist at this time for a specific purpose. My past experiences have shown me that as a soul, I made choices before this current life and these choices propelled me into existence.

It helps me to have a "manifesto" of sorts in order to remind myself of why I am here:

I believe that as an expanded soul, I decided to incarnate in this lifetime. No great entity or god decided for me. I am the god who chose, with Divine love and Divine purpose. I chose my mother, my father, my brother, my aunts, uncles, and cousins, my partners, my husband, my in-laws, my children, my friends, and all the people I have encountered on my path since my arrival on this earth. I believe I chose to be born at exactly 10 minutes after midnight so the planets and stars would support me energetically in a specific way during my human journey, creating patterns for me to tap into. I believe I chose an intellectual father and a free-spirited mother. I believe I chose to not know tenderness and love without conditions as a child. I chose to forget my Divine self until I was 23 so I could embark on the journey of remembering. I chose to not know it in my early life so I could remember it as an adult on my own terms, so I could recognize unconditional love and tenderness, recognize the desire for it within me it, seek it and ask for it, and accept it for myself, by myself, when it was offered to me. I chose to find role models and a culture that would give me the type of environment that would make me self-reliant and push me to seek creative outlets and a deeper meaning to my life. I wisely chose the souls that would support me as well as the ones who would challenge me. I believe I chose peak moments to inspire me and remind me of my path. I chose to give birth to two beautiful angels. Simply by being who they are, they inspire me to play and laugh and be boldly exuberant. I believe they also chose me as a guide in their lives and that my role is to love them for exactly who they are.

I also came with free will—with the ability to change my mind and make decisions along the path. Although there is a grand plan for my existence, I also believe I have the ability to choose at will and change any part of the plan if I desire to. I could have continued to be a teacher if I had really wanted to. I could have stayed with Mike if I had really wanted to. No one was stopping me. But when I chose against my heart and my soul, when I went against what I had originally chosen before my incarnation, life became not as fun, not as easy, and not as meaningful. My only real choice was to remember my destiny or not.

The more I aligned myself with my first choice, my destiny, the more I was aligning myself with the destiny of other heart-centered individuals. More than that, I was aligning with the true heart of individuals who weren't even consciously heart-centered. I could see the spirit of a person beyond their words and actions.

The more I came to remember myself as "god in drag," there was no more conflict or separation between what I wanted and the desires of the entire universe. Deep down inside, we all want the same thing. We just forget, and when we remember, we all have unique ways of expressing it.

In this light, choice takes on a new meaning. When I look back on my life, I can see that I never really had choices, except the perpetual opportunity to choose to remember my true nature or not. When I chose to engage life from *think* and *do* without a solid anchor in *be* and *feel*, I'd forget there was an effortless movement within me, guiding me to express and create my heart's greatest dreams, and I would make choices that would take me out of the flow. But when I chose to remember my essential nature, when I made decisions beyond my intellect, they emerged as a natural choice-less choice coming from my body, my soul, and my divinity.

I am incredibly grateful for my mother. In her presence I am reminded of the importance of that first choice.

CHAPTER 33

MIRRORS AND METAPHORS

—————— • ——————

The soul is an intention. By virtue of its desire to expand and grow, it has a purpose. It is guided by an intelligence. This intelligence communicates in the language of metaphors, and we can decode it if we pay attention to the metaphors abounding all around us, as well as within us. Although metaphors are mostly used as a literary device, I've found that we can discover more of what our soul desires to create, to *do*, through the metaphors that come our way.

I remember the day when I fully realized I could create the life I really wanted—that, after all, I was the field of endless possibilities. For a while, it felt like a huge responsibility. What did I truly want? All the possibilities were at my disposal and all I had to do was choose what I wanted, commit to it, and be patient with it, love it. But how does one choose from the field of infinite possibilities? What I learned was there are choices that are ours to make according to our destiny and the plan we made before we incarnated. Metaphors are the communication system for this plan. We might have the entire field of possibilities at our disposal, but there are clues paving the way to help us find the possibilities that are truly ours.

What is a metaphor? A metaphor is an energy pattern represented in a different way than its primary representation. It is often used to illustrate an abstract pattern in order to make it easier to grasp by presenting the pattern applied in another context. Seeing a metaphor is the act of recognizing the symbolism of that pattern. Metaphors are often used in poetry, like this one from Shakespeare's play *As You Like It*, which gives us a different perspective on life, death, and birth:

> *All the world's a stage,*
> *And all the men and women merely players;*
> *They have their exits and their entrances. . . .*

And Mark Twain's quote on forgiveness:

> *Forgiveness is the fragrance*
> *that the violet sheds on the heel*
> *that has crushed it*

I love metaphors. They are my connection to the great mystery, a map for me to understand the universe's endless forms of expression. When I see the images of outer space captured by the Hubble Telescope, I can't help but notice the incredible resemblance of the landscape of Earth with the landscape of the interior of a human body and the landscape of a single cell.[8] The networks of rivers and streams on Earth's surface mirror the network of nerves and veins throughout our body.

A synchronicity is a creative metaphor, a metaphor showing us in real time the patterns of our trajectory. In the past years that I have led workshops, it never ceases to amaze me how nature outside the workshop room reflects the work we are doing inside. As intensity rises in the conversation and grief and pain are being expressed, pouring rain will come down, mirroring our emotions, as if to support the healing. A deer will catch our eye, a hawk will fly over us, or a majestic rainbow will appear as we surrender to ourselves. By noticing the metaphors offered by the presence of the animals and elements, we witness their medicine and healing powers and realize how connected and not alone we truly are. Nature never ceases to mirror our divinity and our process—it is such a fan and a supporter when we stop long enough to notice and see.

Metaphors were what attracted me to studying literature. I took great pleasure in reading a book and identifying patterns represented in the imagery, structure of the text, narrative, and characters' lives. I loved to deconstruct the patterns and find their meaning in the greater context of the character or the author's life. Now I do the same thing but in my own life. I am curious about patterns and find the meaning within them. I do this for myself and also with my clients and workshop participants.

Metaphors have given me clues about the world, who I am, and why I am here for as long as I can remember. As a child, I was very intuitive. I deeply felt people and situations. I felt how energy patterns came together in a harmonious movement when there was coherence in my environment. I also felt how energy patterns collided and repelled one another when things were being forced or controlled. I often noticed how adults' words would say one thing but the energy they emitted was at odds with those words. But when there was coherence, when there was flow, words spoken were perfect metaphors of the energetic state of that person, and I would respond in delight when it happened.

Looking back on my journey, I can see more metaphors. The word *Maman* was a symbol of closeness with my mother. My watch stopping that night in the restaurant when Mike walked in was a metaphor for my destiny being put on hold.

Surfing was a metaphor for the freedom I experienced in my relationship with Paul, and golfing was a metaphor for control and the measured life I had with Mike.

I now see a metaphor in my liver injury. The liver is the second largest organ after the skin, and it has more known functions than any other organ in the body. Its main functions are to detoxify the blood and process nutrients. Chinese medicine attributes a healthy liver to a healthy relationship with our emotions. It also says when the liver functions optimally, it contributes to a hospitable body for the soul to reside in. My liver splitting down the middle was a metaphor for my two separate realities, my paralleled lives coming to my awareness and needing to integrate.

At the very core, all metaphors can be distilled down to either the pattern of love expanding or being interrupted. On our journey of remembering who we truly are and healing our old wounds, it is useful to notice and become sensitive to the metaphors of love and fear in our life. Love is the unrestrained movement of our life force. Love is spirit flowing through the body and mind, inspiring our every cell to remember its boundless nature. On the other hand, fear is that same movement but interrupted. Fear is when that flow is disrupted and the life force that enlivens us is bound up in protection.

The basis of the work I do with individuals comes from taking a pattern that feels limiting and placing it in a more expanded context. When I am listening deeply, I am looking for the prevalent pattern—the thread that appears limited. Once I feel it and find it, I sense how it could be applied in a more expanded and loving context to free the narrative from the limiting boundaries of fear.

When I use Huna symbols in my energy healing sessions, I work with ancient symbols originating from patterns in nature. They are primary life patterns—patterns that have an expanded intention and can be applied to any situation.

The goal during an energy healing session is to encourage the restricted pattern of energy in the body to relate to a more expanded pattern. If successful, the body recognizes its life force in the pattern, raises its vibration, and attunes to it. One only needs to simply be a witness to the attuning.

I want to share this story with you that I found in Deepak Chopra's *The Spontaneous Fulfillment of Desire*.

A man entered a village and went to see the Sufi master, the wise old man of the village. The visitor said, "I'm deciding whether I should move here or not. I'm wondering what kind of neighborhood this is. Can you tell me about the people here?" The Sufi master said, "Tell me what kind of people lived where you came from." The visitor said, "Oh, they were highway robbers, cheats, and liars." The old Sufi master said, "You know, those are exactly the same kinds of people who live here." The visitor left the village and never came back. Half an hour later, another man entered the village. He sought out the Sufi master and said, "I'm thinking of moving here. Can you tell me what kind of people live here?" Again the Sufi master said, "Tell me what kind of people lived where you came from." The visitor said, "Oh, they were the kindest, gentlest, most compassionate, loving people. I shall miss them terribly." The Sufi master said, "Those are exactly the kinds of people who live here, too."[9]

What this parable illustrates is how our external reality is a metaphor for our internal perception. Sometimes leaving a job we don't like because of the people or the environment is not enough to make us happy or fulfill our soul's desires. Because if unhappiness lives inside, it won't help to change the world outside of us. We will continue to create the same reality.

Relationships are a great source of metaphors. The people in our life are mirrors of what is moving through us. When I looked into Olivier's eyes moments after his birth, I felt warmth and peace in my body and the insight of being in the presence of immense love. The loving essence of my soul recognized itself in him. As Olivier expressed himself without restraint by simply *being* there, whole and beautiful, my being responded by vibrating at the same frequency, eliciting a peak experience.

My daughter, Hanalei, was born screaming at the top of her lungs. It seemed like she had so much to say and share with the world. As she has grown up, the ability to express herself without restraint hasn't left her, and it is my favorite thing about her. When I witness the immensity of her soul as she laughs, dances, and sings freely and feels so deeply with exuberance, I gasp at my soul's desire to sing its song without inhibition. Hanalei is such a force, and she unapologetically expresses that force, boldly shaping her world as she goes.

Our relationships are often our best teachers, especially the challenging ones. Often we wish for the difficult relationships in our life to go away. They drain us and don't seem to add anything of value. But the challenging people in our lives are our mirrors, reflecting the limiting patterns that exist within ourselves. When you become a witness of yourself in other people's words and actions and can see the challenging people simply reflecting aspects of yourself that you don't like, haven't forgiven yourself for, or haven't loved enough, you then hold the power to change that relationship. Instead of feeling attacked or victimized by the person, you can introduce the feeling of being the advocate for a past trauma that lives inside you. You then stand in a position of choice, empowered with the ability to own what is yours and heal what is moving within you. When a difficult conversation arises, instead of looking away, face it (or lean into it). Stay in the hard conversation—present to your discomfort and the "stuff" that is yours. You are not the "stuff," but it does live in you as an uninvited visitor.

When you courageously stay within your own discomfort, with deep breath, attention, and self-love, you will begin to notice that the other person has changed. As you shift and transform, you will emit a different energetic pattern that attracts new, more expanded patterns. The old pattern will dissipate, therefore no longer sending out energy to attract what it used to attract. Instead, a new, more expansive pattern will be present and people who fit that pattern will be drawn to you. Your life will change by virtue of your life within having shifted. You will be in control because you are the creator.

When it comes to the limited aspects of ourselves we notice in others, we can ask the questions: Where does that aspect live in me? Where in my life am I that? Not in a judgmental way, but in the spirit of curiosity and self-discovery. The same goes for when we notice something amazing about another person. When we are inspired by a friend or a role model, a part of us is recognizing ourself in the other. That essence of who we consider them to be lives within us. If we didn't have that pattern within us, we would not be inspired by it. We wouldn't even notice it. When we admire people like Mother Teresa or the Dalai Lama, there is recognition of ourselves in them. We are that love and compassion, and our bodies tell us so.

Spending time with people who inspire us is a good way to evolve into the person we know we are meant to be. If you desire to become a writer, start a writing group and invite writers to join. If you want more artistic expression in your life, go to museums and art galleries and have conversations with art enthusiasts and artists. Engage your curiosity and follow it where it wants to lead you. When you get there, allow yourself to feel enlivened and enchanted. Let that essence guide you to your next bread crumb.

We can ask: "Where does that expanded essence live in me?" and "What are the sensations, the feelings, the images, the colors that come up for me when I am in the experience?"

When you find it, love and nurture it by bringing breath and attention to it. Then ask, "Where am I already that in my life?" See where you are already living this essence or when you used to live this essence. When you find it, purposefully grow that area of your life space, and let go of things that are not part of that essence.

When we accept and love ourselves for being the whole spectrum of expression—the shadow and the light, the fear and the love—we remember that we are whole. We stop judging ourselves for our shortcomings, seeing that they are simply unexamined aspects of ourselves. When we stop judging ourselves, we can then be the mirrors of the soul for another person. All we see in others is the same we know ourselves to be: whole. We can be "compassionate with somebody else's passion" without the constraints of limiting beliefs.[10]

I believe the greatest guides and teachers are those who understand their shadow. They can listen without trying to fix the other person, and the other person can speak without feeling like something is wrong with them. When we understand this, we can become great guides for others, mirroring back honest and unconditional support.

The analogy of the man looking for a new place to live illustrates well the adage: as within, so without. No matter where we find ourselves in time and space, our reality will be the reflection of what is happening inside of us.

So how can metaphors help us find the path of our soul?

When we recognize the patterns of our soul within ourselves—inspiration, awe, exuberance, peace, gratitude, and compassion—we begin to create a reality outside of us that is a reflection of our inner state. When we bring more attention to these patterns, when we feel them and allow them to move through us, to grow, and to be expressed, we create our reality. We act as the mighty creator that we really are.

Soul patterns are different ways in which we experience our soul within ourselves. The soul experience is so subjective, there is no one correct way. Throughout the past 15 years, I have noticed the patterns of my soul have a very different feel than the patterns from my past. The patterns of my soul resonate with my experience of joy, acceptance, laughter, beauty, delight, insight, and growth. The main thread is the sensation of expansion in my chest and knowing in my belly.

When you experience a feeling of expansion within your body, take note. Make a mental note of the physiological experience in your body so you can remember that this is a clue your soul is sending you. Follow these clues one at a time. They will lead to more and more discovery of your calling.

One day, during an exercise in a personal development course I was taking part in, I was invited to choose an element of nature that echoed an aspect of myself. I chose the sun and desired to be more like it. Then an insight dawned on me: I might not simply be "like" the sun, but I could "be" the actual sun. As I considered this thought and put myself into the sun and the sun within me, an insight came crashing down on me. I had to breathe deeply. At first I was terrified of emanating so much light and worried that I might burn the people I loved if I allowed myself to *be* the sun. And then when I took another deep breath into that fear, I knew I was shining a little brighter.

The same thing happens when I hear a good song on the radio and enjoy it so much I feel like crying. Or when I witness skillful actors acting in a great play. I am fully engaged, in complete recognition of the pattern of creating out of feeling. When we drove on the border of Switzerland and Italy, in the presence of the majestic Alps, I cried tears of reverence. When these moments happen, I bring my attention to the feeling of beauty and joy and I breathe deeply into it. I invite the overwhelming feeling of being fully alive to the energy of my soul to take more space in my body, with gratitude. These moments are full of grace. Sometimes I feel it's so much, I am going to burst with the immensity of the feelings. Sometimes I even get scared of the intensity of my joy.

In those moments, I trust that my body can handle this intensity and can process the energy. I know that what I am feeling is the hugeness of my soul and with each breath, I shift my entire body to make more space for it. I know the universe wouldn't send me something I couldn't handle. I know I am getting a gift, an opportunity to rewire my body to be more soul-like in the world. I know that this is how I *become*.

Think about those moments that take your breath away. What is the essence of the moment? What is the energetic signature, the quality of the moment? This essence is the essence of your soul. I see these moments like dots on a dot-to-dot picture, leading us one step at a time, and then all at once, to the whole picture, to the day when we look back and see how all the dots we followed were connected in some intelligent way, forming a whole picture. Our job in the moment is to trust that there is an intelligence and a grand plan at play. All we have to do is trust one subjective experience of awe, of joy, of pure love at a time and let it guide us to the next one.

Knowing this, we can choose to foster an inner landscape of inspiration of whatever our heart desires. We can choose to place our attention on what matters the most and release what does not serve us anymore. We can choose to plant the seeds of childlike play, wonder, and discovery again.

CHAPTER 34

CONSCIOUS
CREATOR

———— • ————

Why am *I* here? Why did *I* choose to come to Earth at this time? What is *my* calling?

Too many die with the regret of not having pondered these questions sooner or more deeply in life. If only we knew the answers, we would know what to focus on and manifest accordingly.

What I have discovered is the answers are not fixed like a particular career or a specific thing we do, but are more of an essence or a process. And this process is often not easily translated into an already-existing paradigm because it is new and creative. So asking is more relevant than answering.

A question in the mind is a ray of light inside a dark room—it helps you to contemplate whether there is something more to this moment than meets the eye. With a question, a door to "another way" appears.

Answering the question right here and right now with our intellectual abilities and logical mind is not as important as pondering it and living it. We can't impose conditioned boundaries and labels on something that is boundless and ever-changing. If we allow ourselves to keep the question in our awareness, in our heart, we will continue to propel ourselves in the direction of the answer.

Living the question is living with intention and purpose. When we ask a question to ourselves, we share with our being and the universe's energetic field our desire to know, understand, and discover more of who we are. When we ask a question without trying to find an answer, we keep our minds open to all possibilities. The more we let go of the timeline for the answer to be revealed and its means of unfolding, the more efficient the asking will be.

A fertile time to plant the seed of a question is right after meditation, whether it is as soon as we awake in the morning or during a peaceful moment we have mindfully carved out for ourselves during our day, because the mind is calmer and the body is in growth mode. During these propitious times, asking a question plants an intention in the fabric of consciousness to being open to what the soul desires to communicate. When the mind and body are quiet and peaceful, the seed is planted in fertile ground.

This is a very different approach to the mind primarily being used to construct an intention. With my mind, I can construct any intentions I want: I want a new house, a new car, world peace, to meet my soul mate, etc. These are not right or wrong, or good or bad. With hard work and time, these can surely be achieved; we are the creator of all of it. But what I have experienced is these intentions might not be in full alignment with my soul. And when they are not, it feels like hard work with the *why* of doing these things not being rooted in a deeper, more meaningful purpose.

When disconnected from the body and the soul, the mind can only re-create what it already knows, therefore re-creating a different version of the past. If you desire to explore something novel, if you desire deep within your soul to know all the dimensions of the creative self and to experience joy on all the levels of existence, your intentions should come from that same deeper and more expanded place of *being*. The intentions then have to be formulated in a more expanded way as well. They need to be formulated in the form of an inquiry.

Often people teach a sort of dissolution of responsibility with intentions, as if you give the universe your request and your work is done. I see this as the giving away of our power to a force that is separate from us with the capability of providing or holding back.

There is a big difference between fully owning what is really meaningful deep within us as a sacred desire and asking the universe to manifest what we intellectually understand our wants to be. When an intention comes from the essence of our most authentic being, it resonates more vulnerably within us. We are more emotionally invested because there is more at stake. Who we are is being fully owned and claimed, and expressing that is a huge step in our evolution. We are essentially honoring that we love ourself and matter enough to validate it through our claiming and expressing of our deepest desires in the world.

Several years ago, during a meditation, a facilitator asked me, "Why are you here?" She didn't offer more details and, for a moment, I couldn't figure out if she meant why was I here in this particular session or why was I here in life in general. The more I considered both possibilities, the more I came to realize the answer might be exactly the same. If this moment is all there is, my choice then is my choice now.

When this insight hit me, time and space collapsed within me and it felt like all of history poured into my body into this singular point in time. If this was true and if I aligned myself with the reason why I was here in this moment in this course, then I would connect with the grander "why" I am here, in this life. They would share the same essence.

My intention for being in the workshop was to remember more of who I truly was and to help others do the same. I wanted to heal, find inner peace, and deepen my relationship with my soul. That was my dharma and my soul's calling. The how and when I did that were just details that would be revealed as I lived my life.

Being the conscious creator is a very different way of manifesting our reality. We invite *be* and *feel* to inform what we *think* and *do*, and for our deepest desires to manifest. It is more of an "allowing" than a "doing"—allowing the flow of the soul to be expressed as opposed to controlling an outcome through action in order to get results. We become artists in the medium of life.

Being the conscious creator doesn't mean that I don't hurt or get lost, because I do! When I am in the depths of my own inner turmoil, I try to remember that I am not the hurt or the story attached to the turmoil. Instead, my body is a vessel for processing it. I try to remember that before the calm, there is the chaos of a storm, and that chaos is the process of life rearranging itself as it transforms and evolves. I try to remember I am in the midst of a creative process, and this is the incubation phase of the process. I try to remember it will pass, like everything in life. I can't hold on to what I used to be because it is disappearing as I heal, and I still don't fully understand who I am becoming. I have come to learn that the more I resist the chaos in my life when it shows up, the more suffering I create for myself. The best thing for me to do is to surrender to the feeling of being out of control and let life do its thing.

CHAPTER 35

AUTHENTIC COMMUNICATION

—————— • ——————

As a very young girl, my heart was my voice. There was no separation. I was exuberant and joyful. I expressed what I felt, with enthusiasm and without restraint. Until little by little, I lost my voice.

In elementary school, I was often in trouble in the classroom. I enjoyed entertaining my friends by turning around and talking to them, telling them funny stories and making them laugh. The teachers didn't like this, but I didn't pay much attention to them. The consequence? A lot of time behind the "time-out" bookshelf with the other troublemakers.

And a lightbulb moment.

I had once again been put in time-out when I suddenly became aware I was the only girl in my class who still got in trouble. I remember looking over at another classmate named Veronique. Her hair was neat, and she wore a beautiful dress that was clean, unlike my jogging suit, which was peppered with mud stains. She sat up straight and listened to the teacher. She was often praised.

In that moment, I decided I'd had enough and I began to pay attention to the teacher and obey. Turns out I was quite good at that. I became one of the best-behaved and highest-achieving students in my class. I loved the feeling of being praised, seen, and validated by the teacher. It felt like love and was certainly much better than being scolded. This was a pivotal moment. I had figured out how to control my environment and therefore control how I felt.

So I stayed with it. I developed the identity of the smart girl and the voice that came with it. The smart girl's voice is not as spontaneous and doesn't come from the heart. It is calculated and measured for a specific outcome. It comes from the mind, where it can be managed.

Eventually, my heart barely spoke. I didn't even know there was another way to *be* but to live from my mind. My voice became controlled for outcomes that my mind wanted. But a tiny little inner voice remained, the one I considered crazy and couldn't make go away.

This pattern of trying to please others through my behavior continued. There was the experience of writing a high school paper about *my* life philosophy, receiving a bad mark, and then rewriting it to please the teacher. Then there was my thesis, where I put more emphasis on what my thesis director wanted, never truly writing what my heart wanted to express.

The pressure of my heart's desire to speak created the pain in my head. Little by little, with the right people in the right space at the right time, I peeled back the layers of the onion that had been keeping a veil between my awareness and my heart. At the beginning, I didn't know there was another way. But when I was reminded of my heart and to go back into my body and listen to the information it was communicating, I gradually found the path to my heart and the ability to reclaim my spontaneous voice.

A few years ago, with the encouragement of a great friend, I joined a community choir. There I could let my heart sing out loud without interrupting its innate impulse to express. Many times, standing in the back row with all these beautiful men and women voicing in harmony, tears of joy would flow down my face. Singing released tension and freed restrictions in my throat, jaw, and lips that I didn't even know I had. My soul had a path to directly express itself in one uninterrupted movement, with passion, purpose, and wisdom.

It has only been recently that I could truly see how much energy I expended in keeping my mouth shut or thinking way too much before I spoke. This resulted in resentment and anger brewing quietly inside me and many hours and days in conversations I had no deep interest in. I had become a chameleon, hiding my true self and only bringing out certain aspects of it in certain situations, like donning a role or a costume.

The idea that showing vulnerability is a weakness has been hardwired in many of us. We hold back, ashamed of our sadness, anger, disappointment, and resentment. It is interesting to note that metaphorically, the throat, which is the instrument with which we express our vulnerability, is located at the neck, the most exposed and unprotected place in the body. I have witnessed in my private practice that true creativity in one's life lives on the lips of one's vulnerability.

In the last few years, the American scholar and author Brené Brown has become famous by sharing her research findings on vulnerability and shame as well as her own personal story of her "breakdown" in her 2010 TED talk. In her books *The Gifts of Imperfection* and *Daring Greatly*, she identifies shame as the reason why we dread being vulnerable with one another. Shame is the fear that connection with others will be taken away, or lost, if they discover a certain aspect of our self.

Many of us have gone through experiences growing up where we experienced judgment, ridicule, or dismissal when we expressed our emotions or vulnerability. When the connection with another valued human being is threatened by the expression of our emotions, a child will choose to keep the connection over expressing their emotions. In essence, the unconscious message conveyed is, "Me, just me being me, spontaneous without restraint, is not enough, is bad, is wrong. I am not enough, I am bad, I am wrong."

Shame is one of the most toxic emotions we can have. Renowned psychiatrist Carl Jung calls it "a soul-eating emotion." Shame is powerful because it is directly linked to our identity. When we feel shame, we feel "less than." We, consciously or unconsciously, identify ourselves with being bad or being wrong.

Shame can lead us into a vicious cycle of circular logic by virtue of having the judgment of a second party involved, whether it is coming from our own judgment of ourselves or the judgment from another person.

Shame exists in silence. This silence fuels our sense of unworthiness and our judgmental thoughts. Underneath it, our truth desires to be expressed, a truth that has been silenced for too long. Putting voice to our shame by speaking our truth, expressing what happened and how we feel, will stop silence from feeding the shame.

One of the most healing things we can do for ourselves is find our group of open-minded and *heart-minded* people and seek out our community of choice, a place where we can speak out loud the truth we carry. They might not be our actual family. We might have to get out of our comfort zone and reach out to different kinds of people who connect with the healing journey we are on. Our world changes when we engage with it differently. What can you do today that will take you out of your own comfort zone?

Putting sound to our deepest emotions restores movement, peace, and joy. Words of shame and words of the heart tend to float around in our heads. They are often looping and not really resolving anything. Allowing the words to collide with sound and emerge outside of our body into the world resolves issues. When sound moves through our throat, passes our vocal cords, and pushes out through our mouth, the unmanifested gets to express itself and becomes manifest.

Traumatic incidents around the neck and face and the repeated shutting down of a young person's opinion and truth can wire the mouth in a way that when we want to speak our truth again as an adult, our lips don't remember how. Can you relate to the experience of feeling an intense emotion welling up in your body and having someone there who deeply cares and wants to support you, but when you try to express yourself, your throat seizes, your tongue feels heavy, and your lips don't seem to work? The words are in your head, but when you try to say them, the sounds won't come out?

We need one another. It is important for us to come together and have authentic conversations where we can reacquaint ourselves with our voice, with the words of our heart, and with compassion and tenderness, in a safe and supportive environment. By witnessing one another with unconditional love, we can allow our words to make their way through and rewire our communication instrument.

It is important to choose our words wisely and with integrity because words create our reality. It is helpful to ask ourselves questions like: Are the words I use reflecting who I really am or who I think I should be? Do my words reflect a conditioned self that has kept me small and from which I am ready to move on? Are the words I speak *my* words or do they belong to someone else living in my head or surfacing from the past?

Speaking our truth takes courage—the courage to acknowledge the story, emotion, or event of the past that is moving inside our body and to follow that impulse and give it substance in the world. Putting sound to our truth while simultaneously being witnessed gives us the permission and the courage to face the unknown, share our dreams, and move through uncharted territory, trusting that we are supported and safe. In that act of making our truth "real" through our voice, our whole organism rewires with this new information. In a single moment, everything within us can change—our cells, our beliefs, our thoughts, and our sense of capability, identity, and safety.

We are social beings. We are naturally designed to share with others our feelings and our experiences, regardless of if we are introverted or extroverted. We desire to communicate in the same way our organs communicate with one another for optimal functioning, growth, and survival.

When I express myself, I make a choice. I plant a seed of intent. If we want our lives to change, we should consider changing our conversations.

For this, my mother has been my greatest teacher. Every time I am with her, I get to have a different conversation. I am able to communicate authentically with the one person where communication has been altered. As she grows more and more into her own tenderness, I discover conversations that would never have been possible in the past. And I discover aspects of myself I had not known before. She is a gift to me.

One thing you can easily change in your language that will greatly affect your sense of personal power is not beginning sentences with *I have to.* . . . When we say *I have to do this* or *I have to be like that*, we imply there is some external factor to which we are subject. If we say, "I have to go to work this morning," but don't feel like it, it enables us to defer our responsibility onto "work" or our employer or our life circumstances, when, in fact, we are the author of the situation. It separates us from the decision that we, and only we, have to make, whether consciously or unconsciously.

Instead of saying *I have to go to work*, try saying *I want to go to work*. Even if you don't feel like it in the moment, somewhere along the way, you had wanted this job. If it doesn't feel like that anymore, become real with yourself and look at the "why" and "what" you can change. When you do so, you will come to another crossroad. You may realize that this job is actually the best option right now and make the choice to continue to go to work, at least for now. You are expressing your want. It is empowering to know that you made that decision and you are not at the mercy of external factors or the victim of an unfair world.

Every time you say *I have to*, change it to *I want to*. See how differently it feels and where it leads you in your exploration of your desires. Own your choices. The more you do, the more you will see doors opening. Energetically, the universe will support you and experience you as an active player who is in charge of their destiny.

You are the creator of all. When you recall that truth, deep within yourself, you experience that truth more and more on this Earth at this time. You become the conscious creator.

CHAPTER 36

SAME SOURCE, DIFFERENT POINTS OF ENTRY

———— • ————

Richard, a physician, read all the books he could possibly read on the topic of living a spiritual life. He was a very smart man, and there was very little that he didn't intellectually understand. He could comprehend the depths of quantum physics and the complexity of the ancient Vedic texts without any problems. Yet, he was deeply unhappy. He had a number of addictions, had gambled away his savings, and smoked heavily, and when things got uncomfortable at home, he would escape in his car and drive for days. He didn't understand how, with all the spiritual truths he had studied, his life wasn't peaceful or fulfilling. He decided he couldn't live like that anymore.

When he first came to me, we talked about connecting with the suppressed emotions in his body. This was a foreign concept to him. He believed that talking about his emotions on a logical level was "doing" emotional work. Over the course of his first weekend workshop, we went deep with my version of "doing" the work: identifying where the emotion lives in the body and sitting with the process and discomfort. He nearly ran for the exit! However, little by little, after a few more programs and coaching sessions, he was able to become aware of the emotional body that lived underneath his intelligent head. He learned to trust his body below the neck, and as he processed his emotions, he began to recognize the gateway to the inner peace he so deeply craved. He understood the difference between knowledge and wisdom.

There are different points of entry on the spiritual path, and they are all valid in their own way. For Richard, it was knowledge and intellect. Because spirituality is so subjective, it is important to recognize there is no rightness or wrongness, and one truth doesn't validate or diminish another. We all come home in the end, no matter how we get there. So please be kind, gentle, and generous with yourself and your fellow seekers.

It is important to trust our own unique experience while not indulging the temptation to seek validation from others or compromising our own truth in order to validate someone else's. Everyone needs to do that on their own.

Most often, we enter the path through an external source. We see a gifted psychic, and we open our minds to deeper levels of awareness. We receive a healing from a Reiki practitioner and we feel better, different. We meet a guru, and the love we experience makes us commit to a spiritual life. We read a book that completely changes the way we think. We have a conversation with someone that inspires us to seek more. We take a workshop that changes how we live. We lose someone dear to us, and it pushes us to reconsider what makes our life worth living.

Although the first steps are important, the key is to keep moving inward on the path, to bring the journey back into the body, finding validation within. It is when we try to stay within one externally referenced dogma and when we become attached to the narratives and figures of truth that we end up stuck, giving meaning and power to something outside of us. Ultimately, truth is an experience within us.

My work as a guide and facilitator has made me keenly aware that no two people are at the same place in their journey. I don't mean this in the sense of a spiritual road race or hierarchy—it's more of an appreciation of the different entry points that line the path and that we are all heading in the same direction, just using different roads to get there. I'll share a few more anecdotes from my practice to illustrate what I mean.

Patricia had dedicated her life to helping others as her way of living a spiritual life. She was raised Catholic and had been taught being selfless and of service to those in need was the right thing to do. "Helping others" was the identity she adopted early on as the oldest daughter helping her mother take care of her siblings. This identity kept her from acknowledging her own needs, which were rarely met. Because her self-concept and her self-esteem had long become wrapped up in taking care of others, when the people she helped were no longer there or in need of her, she was left with an existential crisis. She became unhappy and depressed, and had a difficult time finding meaning in her life. Her self-work that would lead her toward a more spiritual life included giving herself the permission to discover what her needs and passions were. She had to consciously work at caring for herself.

For **Janet**, the concept of spirituality was experienced solely from an esoteric perspective. This included a lot of shamanic journeying and taking hallucinogenic substances like ayahuasca. The feeling of bliss that the higher realms offered was very attractive, but it was difficult for her to integrate these experiences into her regular life. Frequently repeated sha-manic rituals and experimentation with various mind-altering substances had resulted in an awareness anchored in another realm, not of her body or here on Earth. These experiences were never integrated into her life or her emotional or physical body, and as a result, she had difficulty functioning and needed help with basic things like managing her career and navigating relationships with other humans. After the highly anticipated year 2012 came and left, she revealed the following: "I didn't plan past 2012. I was sure we would all be ascended by now and that we would live as spiritual beings here on Earth. Now I need help with living in this world." For Janet, the self-work for integrating the spiritual realms into her life included fully feeling pain and traumas that had kept her from being in her body in the first place.

For **Anthony**, it was similar. The past physical and emo-tional traumas in his life had been so great that when he discov-ered the etheric realms, he became addicted to living outside of his body. Over the years, he developed persistent chronic pain, and when he came to me, his body hurt so much that it took many sessions to reenter his emotional and physical body. But with the help of other bodywork such as osteopathy and tradi-tional Chinese medicine treatments, as well as talk therapy, the pain slowly began to go away.

I believe many problems are created when spirituality is considered to exist outside the body and an individual's being. The key is to bring the process back inside ourselves. It is not always comfortable, but it is the way to an embodied spiritual-ity, one that is grounded, genuine, authentic, and empowering.

Eckhart Tolle frequently writes about the great importance of inner body awareness when exploring a spiritual life. In his 2014 book *The Power of Now*, he says: "The fact is that no one has ever become enlightened through denying or fighting the body or through an out-of-body experience. Although such an experience can be fascinating and can give you a glimpse of the state of liberation from the material form, in the end you will always have to return to the body, where the essential work of transformation takes place." Like so many of my clients, once I became honest with the emotions that lived in my body, began to share them, and allowed myself to be vulnerable, I began to truly live out my spirituality, in an integrated way. I connected with a deeper inner peace.

My personal experience with this inner work was messy. We have to lean into the chaos and allow the body to do its thing. Transformation doesn't take place in a linear or logical manner. Like the goop in a chrysalis, it's a mess of repressed emotions, limiting patterns, discomfort, vulnerability, energetic fields, chakras, cellular memories, quantum healing, and more! A leap of faith is required because the healing happens with a greater speed and power than the mind can comprehend. The stakes are high, and the reward is worth the risk.

I believe spirituality is meant to be lived not only on a mountaintop or blissed out in an ashram or solely learned through texts or sermons. It is meant to be embodied moment to moment, in our everyday life, with the messy kitchen in the morning getting the kids off to school, around the dinner table at Christmas with our in-laws, with the back pain that has been nagging at us for years, and with the guilt and shame that sometimes take over our thoughts and demand to be felt.

Spirituality is life. All of life is spiritual. The journey is about meeting ourselves. An embodied spirituality is lived through and through—through our bodies, our minds, our words, our actions, and all the messy bits that are present.

Be Feel Think Do:
Be now with the soul in the body,
Feel now the soul through the body,
Let your soul and your body *Think,*
Let your soul and your body *Do.*

The first step is acceptance. Acceptance of where we find ourselves exactly at this moment. Acceptance of the state of our body, acceptance of the state of our mind, acceptance of the state of our life, with bold honesty. An embodied spirituality begins with the intimate and sincere acceptance of all parts of us, now.

CHAPTER 37

SELF-LOVE AS AN ACT OF SERVICE

W e all know how good it feels to help alleviate another person's suffering. In fact, it can give us feelings of deep connection and oneness. But in order to be able to give to others, we must remember what it is to love ourselves and take care of our own bodies, minds, and hearts.

As individuals, we truly matter. Traditional religion has not necessarily reinforced that idea, but as it turns out, when we know we deeply matter as an individual, and we know this through and through, we can serve the world with our gifts in more powerful ways than if we sacrificed our heart's desires.

I have come to know with such certainty that if we don't care for and love our own hearts and our own self first, we can't care for and love others in a sustainable, healthy, and deep way. The quality of our relationships directly depends on the quality of the relationship we have with ourselves.

When we are happy, it's contagious. It inspires others. It might feel selfish to consider the relationship we have with ourselves as the primary relationship in our lives, but I am not talking about stroking and validating the ego here. I am talking about softening our heart and our often-judgmental mind to our own emotions, feelings, past experiences, and circumstances. I am talking about treating yourself the way you would treat a precious child in your care. This kind relationship with our own deep self informs all the other relationships. It informs not only our sense of happiness, but it affects the happiness of the people around us as well.

Tending to the primary relationship with ourselves is self-love. It is a demonstration of appreciation for the life that moves through us. It doesn't take anything away from others. On the contrary, it inspires. The founders of the great religions found themselves alone and facing their own needs and suffering, even if it meant they would have to leave their families. Buddha spent years in isolation in the forest tending to that inner knowing, and Jesus left his family and community to spend 40 days in the desert confronting his demons. They, too, had to do the emotional self-exploration work in order to be true to their heart, their soul, and their reason for existing! In turn, they helped countless people find the path to peace, and their message continues to impact humanity. They weren't born enlightened. What they greatly desired for the world, they had to find within themselves first.

There is a way that all true needs can be met. No one has to be denied love in order for another person to receive it. This kind of love and connection, this soul love, is a bottomless well!

Sometimes the desire to tend to someone else's happiness regardless of our own conceals the fact that we are frightened to look at ourselves and our own desires. It feels much easier to tend to another's needs. Tending to another's needs can be a distraction from our own discontentment. We are all better parents, friends, caretakers, lovers, and leaders if we make the time to look at our discomfort, do the emotional healing work on ourselves, and nurture that primary relationship.

Loving ourselves is a demonstration of love toward our families, our communities, and our world. It is a demonstration of gratitude for the life we have been given and the incredible gift of the ability to create the reality we want.

With our primary needs already fulfilled, the responsibility is on us to deepen our sense of worth and anchor within ourselves an unshakable sense of safety. This way we can *be feel think do* a new (ancient) way of serving humanity, one that is deeply connected to the needs of our heart and soul's purpose, and therefore connected to the needs at the heart of humanity, to the purpose of the collective soul. In this way, serving becomes a way of living. And it starts with our own sense of worthiness.

For many of us, knowing that we are enough, that we are worthy of love, is perhaps the most difficult step on the spiritual path. We were taught that putting others first is the right and honorable thing to do. But what we weren't taught is that sacrificing our own joy and fulfillment doesn't help anyone in the long run. Taking care of ourselves, asking for help, accepting help, and sharing our emotions is not selfish. It is a critical part of being a fully engaged human being who can actually be of service to others. Self-care is not vanity or from the ego. It's an expression of deep gratitude for our life.

How long can we be of service if we are tired, sick, or overwhelmed? How long will our mental, emotional, and physical health support and provide us with boundless energy if we are not kind and generous with our bodies, our minds, and our hearts? It becomes a vicious cycle we can't get out of if we don't take the time to heal ourselves and connect with our inner peace and joy. The truth is that others will benefit from our disposition much more if we take care of ourselves than if we are martyrs.

I like the metaphor of the oxygen masks on a plane. Without putting your own mask on first, you would not be able to be there to help your child or dependent. If you desire deep self-love for an individual, the best way to impart it is by modeling it. You love others when you model how to love yourself through your state of being, your words, and your behaviors. That is true love. It is deep and rooted, strong and open. It is universal, and it is boundless.

When we practice self-love with Divine love and direct this powerful energy toward our own heart, we gain access to an unlimited spiritual energy supply. Spiritual energy never runs out. We can give much more to others if we are giving with a full tank. By tapping into our own deep well of love and spiritual energy, we can listen and be present to another person so much more than if we were sick, tired, disconnected, disenchanted, and jaded.

Self-love is living with our attention within our body, moment to moment, feeding the body long, deep breaths. It is carving out a time every single day to be alone with ourselves for breath, silence, and prayer or meditation. It is saying, "I know I heal and feel more grounded when I meditate. This is of great value to me. The state of my inner being matters to me the most."

Self-love is saying to the hurt little girl or boy from the past that lives within us, "I am here. I see you. I've got you. We are in this together. What do you need? How can I support you?" When our knee or back hurts, self-love says, "Hey there, I see you. It hurts, doesn't it? Well, I'm here. Tell me more. What do you need?" When we spiral out of control and get overwhelmed with frustration or the feeling of being completely lost, we can do the same thing. We can talk to ourselves like this: "Hey there. I see that you are feeling lost. I am so sorry this is happening to you. How can I help you? What do you need right now?"

Self-love is taking a step back after we have done something we regret and having compassion and forgiveness for ourselves. It is saying, "I am human, I made a mistake, and I am doing my best. Next time I will know to be more present to my inner state."

Self-love is choosing the relationships we want and letting go of the ones that are unhealthy. It is saying, "Living my soul and expressing with authenticity is a priority, and I want to surround myself with people who support me." When a situation turns from uncomfortable to abusive, leaving is self-love. It is saying, "I matter. My emotional safety is a priority right now. I don't want to have to shut down and harden myself to be able to stay in this situation. Compromising my ability to fully feel my heart is not worth it." We can get our strength from our family of choice—we can love ourselves enough to know that we are worthy of being in their company and well worth their time and attention.

Self-love is knowing who to be vulnerable with and when. Living the soul doesn't mean sharing our heart with everyone all the time. It's not always helpful, and sometimes can be more hurtful than anything. Sharing our heart with vulnerability and courage with the people who can meet us where we are is much more supportive than attempting to connect with someone who can't connect with us in an open and nonjudgmental space. I like to discern the moments when expressing vulnerability won't add to my growth. I can tell when certain situations will most likely shake up my own sense of inner safety, and I back away.

If we look closely, we engage in self-abuse quite often in the way we speak to ourselves, choosing to believe the voice of the conditioned mind, judging ourselves for those choices, and staying in situations that are not nurturing and supportive. Here are a few questions to ponder. They are intended to be asked with curiosity, not with judgment.

- How do I speak to myself? Notice the tone with which you address yourself and the words you use in your inner dialogue. We often don't take the time to stop and listen to the inner dialogue on loop in our mind; we have gotten so used to the chatter and the automatic responses to the chatter. A good exercise is to sit quietly, quiet the mind for a minute or two by anchoring your attention within your body, and wait for a thought to arise. When the first one does, write it down. Quiet the mind again with your breath and attention in the body, and write down the next thought when it arises. After 20 thoughts, stop. Reread and notice the themes and tone of the thoughts. How do you speak to yourself? Is there a pattern? Is there a hidden belief behind those thoughts of *I am not worthy*, *I am not enough*, or *I will always fail*? Inquire with playful curiosity and stay with the feelings in the body that the questions bring up. Breathe into them and follow their movement until you feel more ease. This is practicing self-kindness.

- How quickly do you judge or doubt yourself when something goes wrong? In other words, do you give yourself the permission to make mistakes? We are so quick at putting ourselves down. It might not be something we express out loud, but notice the speed at which your thoughts jump to blame, guilt, or shame when you perceive that you have failed. A good practice is to notice the thoughts before believing them fully. Then, with a smile and without judgment, you can say to yourself, *Look at me being hard on myself again. How interesting!* The simple act of observing starts to soften the edges of the conditioned beliefs. This is practicing self-compassion.

- Where in my life do I stay in abusive conversations, relationships, or situations? We often pride ourselves in being able to handle a lot, or in being good listeners, especially if our work is about supporting others. The person doing the abusing is indeed responsible for their behavior. There is no doubt about that. Even so, at some point, we are responsible for our behavior. When we have a choice to leave, and when we choose to stay in an abusive situation, we are abusive to ourselves. We are not practicing self-love. Speaking our truth, asking for what we need, removing ourselves from a situation, and giving ourselves some space is self-love. It's not weakness. I find this happens the most with employers, parents, siblings, and spouses, where we feel we don't have a choice but to be in the relationship or stay out of fear of losing the love of a family member or our financial security. (We usually don't purposefully hang out with friends who are bullies.) Can you be kind enough to stand up for yourself in those situations? Nobody else can do it for you in the way you can. This is self-advocacy.

- Do I give priority to my heart and my soul every day? Now is the time for your life. Not tomorrow, and no, it's not too late. You did not miss the boat when you were younger. That is the amazing thing about our soul: it is eternally there, and it is up to us to tune in and connect.

If we don't, it will still be there, shining and
lovingly waiting for us to pay attention when we
are ready. Like the sun in Hafiz's poem: "Even
after all this time, the Sun never says to the
Earth, 'You owe me.' Look what happens with
a love like that. It lights the whole sky." What
do you do each day to make connecting with
and expressing your soul a priority? Meditating,
journaling, authentic conversations, yoga,
running, singing, dancing, playing with your
kids, full-body conscious breathing? How do you
engage your joy and your peace every day? Make
it a priority! If you don't, then who will? If not
now, then when?

I boil it down to these four ideas: acceptance, commitment, patience, and self-love. The *acceptance* of all parts of
us—the good, the bad, and the ugly; the *commitment* to keep
the faith and not give up even when it feels like we took a
giant step backward; the *patience* to not worry about how and
when; and the *self-love* to know that we are worth the journey.
Our birthright is that we are infinite, creative beings of love,
and our emotional body deserves to heal.

*When you love who you are, there is no thing
unconquerable, no thing unreachable. When you truly
love yourself, you live only in the light of your own
laughter and travel only the path of joy . . . that light—
that united force, that happiness, that jolliness, that
mirthful state of being—extends itself to all humanity.*[11]

— RAMTHA

CHAPTER 38

LIVING FEARLESSLY

——— • ———

The more that time passes, the more we tend to look back on our lives and assess all we have experienced and accomplished. Did we achieve what we set out to do? Did we realize our dreams? Did we express our feelings or keep them inside? Did we acknowledge our true desires or ignore them?

According to Bronnie Ware, author of the 2011 book *The Top Five Regrets of the Dying: A Life Transformed by the Dearly Departing*, we all go through a series of emotions in the last 6 to 12 weeks of our life. Too often, these emotions include a lot of regret. Ware sums up the regrets in these five statements:

1. I wish I'd had the courage to live a life true to myself, not the life others expected of me.

2. I wish I hadn't worked so hard.

3. I wish I'd had the courage to express my feelings.

4. I wish I had stayed in touch with my friends.

5. I wish I had let myself be happier.

Ware's top five regrets all point to the importance of knowing oneself. If you don't know who you really are, how can you live an authentic life? If you don't know what makes you happy, how can you have more happiness?

Knowing that one day you may look back on your life and you may have regrets, consider asking yourself now how you want to feel on the day you are faced with your mortality. Why are you here on this Earth and what is your desired state of being at the end of your life, when you transition back to your innate essence as spirit?

We can influence that moment by pondering this question now. Imagine you are celebrating your 98th birthday. All your friends are there to honor you and the extraordinary life you began to live the day you decided to live from your soul. You remember that day. You made a commitment to yourself to fully feel the extent of your soul and to live an authentic life connected to your heart. On that day, you knew that first step would lead you to where you are now as a content, fulfilled, and joyful 98-year-old.

Listen carefully to your heart. Right now. Is there a dream you've been harboring that won't let you go? Are there desires asking to be born? Your heart will tell you. Trust what it says. Trust yourself. What is the dream you may have convinced yourself to be impossible, but it keeps resurfacing? And when you envision the dream in your mind's eye, does it make your heart overflow with joy and love?

*If one advances confidently in the direction
of his dreams, and endeavors to live the life which
he has imagined, he will meet with a success unexpected
in common hours.*

— HENRY DAVID THOREAU

What we put our attention on will grow. Advancing confidently in the direction of our soul's dream, following the bread crumbs of peak experiences, and paying attention to the metaphors along the way will lead us to that dream—not in the way and with the timeline we envision, but in ways we can't foresee.

Living our life in this manner is living fearlessly. It takes courage to be on the path of healing and becoming all we can be. It can be hard and isolating at times. After we've committed and before our community of choice shows up, we often find ourselves alone, standing in the truth of what we know. We must trust that even if our minds can't fully see the path ahead, even if no one seems to be there for us, the path is there and we are supported. Trusting like this requires us to conquer our fear of the unknown and our fear of judgment from others and to express boldly and without restraint the truth in our hearts. The word *courage* can seem unspiritual, but in her first book, Brené Brown points out its origin:

> *Courage* is a heart word. The root of the word *courage* is *cor*—the Latin word for heart. In one of its earliest forms, the word *courage* meant "To speak one's mind by telling all one's heart." Over time, this definition has changed, and today, we typically associate courage with heroic and brave deeds. But in my opinion, this definition fails to recognize the inner strength and level of commitment required for us to actually speak honestly and openly about who we are and about our experiences—good and bad. Speaking from our hearts is what I think of as "ordinary courage."[12]

By my grandfather's hospital bed, and later by his grave, there were yellow flowers. This is my very first memory. I was four years old. We had made the long drive down the south shore of the Saint Laurent River to be with him in his final days. When I saw him I was joyous. I don't remember feeling sad. I felt happy to be with him. Even though I knew he would die, I was excited for his journey ahead, even though I didn't comprehend it. This was a big contrast to the overall mood in the hospital room. The energy was confusing.

My father and his siblings were obviously very sad, but it wasn't the kind of sadness I was used to. What I remember is that the words the adults around me spoke didn't match their feelings inside. I can understand now there was a dissonance between how they felt, which I could feel and tap into as truth inside myself, and how they spoke to one another and to me. It all felt like a lie. For the first time I was aware of my separation from people, what Jean-Paul Sartre refers to as *l'autre* or "the other."

Why is this event my first memory? What makes a memory the first one? I wonder if the intensity of emotions around me had something to do with it. I wonder if our first awareness of self as separate, of our "otherness," is what creates our first memory. Because before that, I don't think I needed to be concerned with how others lived their lives. But when the dissonance between their feelings and their words were imposed upon me, I had an opportunity to look outside myself for a truth and perspective other than my own. On that day I unconsciously decided the truth of my subjective experience was up for debate. And a limiting belief was born. And you know the rest of the story!

Our truth is not up for debate. It's nonnegotiable and doesn't need justification from anyone. Our truth is exactly how we kinesthetically and emotionally experience our memories, our present moment, and all our projections and fears about the future. When we put our truth up for debate, we move up into our heads, and we close ourselves to healing, insights, and creativity. We lose our connection to our inner power and spiritual force. We involve an external source in the discussion, the voice that influenced the pattern in the first place.

We are invited now, more than any other time in history, to fully show up in our bodies and in our lives and have the courage to live in a way that is true to our hearts while sharing our fears, emotions, creativity, and spiritual expansiveness with the world in big and small ways.

Living fearlessly means modeling a spiritual life as opposed to preaching a spiritual life. A few years ago, I had the privilege and the joy to get to know Dr. David Simon, co-founder of the Chopra Center, who passed away in 2012. David was a gentle and loving soul who could dispel judgment and fear with very few words. He had the energy of a wise old sage sitting on a mountaintop, yet he very much lived in this world. He walked his talk all the way to the end of his life, never letting the fear of the death of his body come into his awareness and disturb his inner strength and knowing. I know he helped a lot of people in the program room the day he answered this participant's question: "Every time I return home after these great expansive experiences, it never goes well. I try to explain to my husband what happened, how it made me feel. Most of the time I can't find the words that come close to describing the experience. Instead of being understanding and open, he shuts down and seems to feel threatened by my newfound inner freedom. When the opportunity shows up for me to attend another program, he is not so happy about it. My question is: How do I explain to the people I love what the heck happens in these courses and how can I reintegrate gracefully into my family?"

I had asked myself that question many times. When I began my healing work, it was difficult to integrate what I was learning into my life. There always seemed to be a struggle between two seemingly separate worlds: my spiritual life and my "real" life.

David's answer said it all so simply. "Tomorrow, when you arrive at your home, the very first thing you do after opening the door and putting your bags down is to find your husband and make sweet love to him. I promise you, he will get it and he will let you come back anytime you want."

What better way to illustrate the deep Divine love you are experiencing than to put it into practice. To *be* that love. Choosing being love over being right in an argument takes courage; engaging from the heart matters more than being right or having our thoughts validated. When in doubt, choose love. Always. Love is always the answer.

In any given moment, you get to choose to let your heart and your soul speak for you, to express through you. When you do, and when you stay with the difficult conversations and breathe into the discomfort of being vulnerable to yourself or to another person, you practice being whole. You integrate all the scattered pieces of yourself and you bridge the gap between your inner and outer worlds. You make your spirit "real" for yourself and everyone to witness and experience. You embody your spirituality. You boldly model what living in alignment of soul, emotions, thoughts, words, and action looks like. You become the catalyst for change.

AFTERWORD

Finding Father

"**C**an we get some?"

How can you say no to Wayne Dyer? We pull the car over on the Trans-Canada Highway. I'm concerned this is too risky. I tell Paul to stay where he is, that we can find another way.

"Nothing bad can happen, Anne, I am with Wayne Dyer!"

"That's right," Wayne says from the passenger seat. "And anyway, you are eternal!"

As transport trucks whiz by, Paul dodges four lanes of speeding traffic, gets into the bushes, climbs up a lilac tree, and brings back an armful of lilac branches for Wayne.

It's late May 2015, and Paul and I have picked up Wayne and Maya, Wayne's longtime personal assistant and close friend in Ottawa to drive them back to Montreal and then on to Moncton for what would be our last two events together.

Wayne had noticed lilac trees in full bloom on the side of the highway. He shared with us how special they were to him, how they used to grow on his street where he grew up in Detroit and reminded him of his mother. He even recited a few lines of the poem "When Lilacs Last in the Dooryard Bloom'd" by Walt Whitman.

> When lilacs last in the dooryard bloom'd,
> And the great star early droop'd in the western sky in the night,
> I mourn'd, and yet shall mourn with ever-returning spring.
>
> Ever-returning spring, trinity sure to me you bring,
> Lilac blooming perennial and drooping star in the west,
> And thought of him I love.

They would be the first and the last lilacs we would see on this long trip. An oasis of flowers in a sea of poplar and pine.

The car smelled amazing and Wayne was so happy. He kept them in his room for his entire stay in Montreal. The fragrance that powerfully filled the car that day symbolizes to me so vividly the Divine love that emanated from this man.

In the five years before his passing, I was blessed with several opportunities to spend time with this enlightened teacher and got to know him better. The recognition I felt on the first day I saw him on Kauai grew deeper and deeper and made space for a mentor-mentee relationship as well as a beautiful friendship. I learned so much from Wayne simply by being in his presence. But as I reflect back on our time together, nearly one year after his transition, I realize he came into my life to help me heal my relationship with the masculine. Let me explain.

That weekend in Montreal I was to speak for a few moments before Wayne took the stage, presenting on the premise of this book. I was unusually nervous—so much so that the stress translated into a pretty nasty cold. I had spoken in front of large crowds before, but this time it felt different. I was presenting something that was very sacred to me, I was really vulnerable, *and*, to make matters worse, I was doing it in front of my mentor.

The morning of the presentation, my emotions were getting the better of me. I felt a fire in my solar plexus. I couldn't remember the last time I felt this insecure. I meditated and asked myself, *Why am I so afraid?* As I took a deep breath, I became aware of an acute desire to make Wayne proud. I was looking for his approval. The more I connected to this truth within, the more I felt myself as a little girl, yearning for her father to see her and acknowledge her. I sat with this feeling for a few moments. Then I took another deep breath and connected with the energy of my father. As I exhaled, I felt a sadness within me. An ancient sadness, one of a little girl desperately needing her father's love. I thought to myself, *These are daddy issues! I had no idea!*

In my childhood memories, my father is a reserved, quiet, and debilitatingly shy man, always showing up in the backdrop, never an active player. He was overshadowed by my extroverted mother's larger-than-life personality. I don't remember my father taking a stand on much or having an opinion about our upbringing. His silence, however, left a trace.

I always knew, deep down in my heart since I was very young, that my father truly believed in me and saw me for who I really was. I know now that he always saw himself in me and trusted me, but when push came to shove, he would always defer to my mother. But like all humans, we often deal with emotions we don't understand. How can we support another human being if we struggle with supporting ourselves? How can we reflect the Divine spark to another if we don't know how to honor our own? In moments where I wanted an advocate for who I was, my father's impulse to stay quiet was stronger than his impulse to take a stance, to speak his own truth.

I deeply love my father. We have a beautiful relationship today, one in which we support each other on the respective paths we have chosen. I know he loves me deeply, and he tells me this often.

The desire to be supported by the masculine has played itself out many times in my life, often in unhealthy ways, showing up as fabricated dramas, insecurities, and manipulation. I can see now how the insecurities that came up based on the need to be validated were often stronger than my ability to stand up for who I knew I was. But my body remembered and always tried to keep me safe from hurt, this time in the form of a cold for three days that threatened to cancel my participation in the event.

As all these insights began pouring in, I consciously released the sadness, knowing it would ground me even more in my self, my truth, my heart. Every exhalation gave way to an increased sense of inner assurance as the fear and need to be validated diminished. I began to feel "father" within me, as opposed to outside of me—the masculine in me was rising up to meet the task at hand, supportive and loving.

As I walked into the venue, I noticed a man walking toward me in the hallway. Much to my surprise, my father had made the three-hour trip to come see the show. He hugged me, and I felt like a little girl, safe and loved. Another wave of release washed over me as he held me. I gave him his front-row ticket, the one I had reserved just in case, right beside Wayne.

Opening for Wayne Dyer is no cakewalk. People are there to see *him*, and as an unknown entity, I have mere moments to win them over and make an impression. As I was standing behind the curtain, about to step in front of 1,500 people, my speaking coach, Nancy, without knowing anything about my morning contemplation, whispered to me, "Just imagine you are in your father's arms—and speak from that place of total support and safety." So out I stepped, supported by the father energy inside me and my father's energy in the front row, feeling completely safe and empowered to serve everyone else in the room.

The show was brilliant. If you asked people who were in the audience that day, they would tell you Wayne was transcendent and luminous. He sat down in the chair and began speaking as if we were all gathered in his private living room having an intimate conversation with a great master. It was such a gift.

Later that evening, at a post-event reception, a man approached Wayne with an unusual gift. His name was Martin, and he took remarkable pictures of orbs and elementals. In addition, he often received clear messages from spirits, including specific instructions regarding his photos. A somewhat reluctant participant in this journey, he was halfway through the task of delivering framed pictures of a particular entity to five specific people around the world.

At first glance, it seemed to be a photograph of an orb of light framed in a wooden triangle. But an accompanying letter explained it was Dr. Jose Valdivino, an entity channeled through John of God, whom Wayne had credited with healing his leukemia some years prior.

On the back of the frame was a note from Martin, and at the bottom, he had signed it with a drawing of a blue butterfly. Wayne told me this was significant. He had told a very special person in his life that he would communicate with her after he passed, coming to her as a blue butterfly. The photograph struck Wayne as powerful and important, although he wasn't fully sure what to make of it. The next day he spent several hours with Martin, discussing the entities, the photograph, and trying to discern the meaning of it all.

On the day of our event in Moncton, I came to see Wayne in his hotel room for our routine morning meditation in front of the orb. He looked pale and tired. He told me he had sweats all night and felt like the entities were working on him. He went on to give another incredible show that evening.

A few weeks later, I found myself in a Maui restaurant with Wayne and a few of his friends. We were having dinner after the Writing from the Soul workshop. Nancy Levin, a teacher I truly admire, was sitting beside me, and we began to talk about the power of radical openness in our healing process. I am not sure how we came onto the subject of fathers, but I said to Nancy that I felt lucky to have a husband who was physically affectionate and demonstrative of love with our kids because I hadn't experienced that with my father. I shared my desire to give more kisses and hugs to my dad. I was not aware Wayne was listening in until he looked at me as if nobody was there and said, "Oh, Anne, I so wish I had been your father." There were a few seconds of silence around the table. In that moment, I felt in some strange way he knew he had been helping me heal that day in Montreal.

Two months later, his heart stopped working, sending shock waves around the world. No one saw it coming—he was healthier than he had been in years and was so full of life.

I still see the text message in my mind's eye: "Have you heard the news about Wayne?" I can still see his Facebook page, mushrooming with confusion, questions, disbelief. I started to feel ill. I was sure it was a cruel prank and that his account had been hacked. I called Maya. She was in tears, and that is when it hit me, with an impact that felt like my insides were being crushed. I did not have a reference point for grieving a loss like this one. It physically hurt.

Paul, Olivier, Hanalei, and I huddled close and cried together. We all loved him. My children knew him as an exceptionally kind person who would turn the boredom of hanging out backstage into a giggling gong show filled with jokes, stunts, and gifts. To see Wayne around children was to witness grace in action, a culmination of a lifelong pursuit of spiritual truths revealed in a state of complete presence with youthful play. Hanalei missed him acutely; there went the man who knew a good cartwheel when he saw one.

I held his memory in my mind's eye, obsessively replaying the last few times we had been together and all the details of our conversations. I was scared that if I forgot, I would lose him for good. I felt isolated by my sadness and, for a little while, I felt I had lost my purpose. I wondered why any of the work we did even mattered. The world had been robbed of its brightest light, an enlightened teacher, at a time when we needed him the most. I felt that without him, there was little hope for a healed world. I didn't know if I was capable of keeping this passionate spark I had for healing and soul realization if he wasn't there to lead the way.

A few mornings later, I woke up with his words in my head: *Instead of asking, "What is in this for me?" always ask, "How may I serve?"* Quietly within, I began to repeat this phrase and brought the question to my heart as an offering. In that moment, I felt an opening and expansive feeling in my chest. I gasped at the sensation of rushing water filling my body. I needed to let go of the images and dialogues I was keeping in my mind and allow the feeling of my love for him into my heart. The more I allowed myself to feel the love, the more I felt it coming back to me in return, more than I had ever felt before in a meditation. I knew then it wasn't the memories that were going to keep him alive—it was the love between us that would. Just as with the night Granny passed away, I realized my relationship with Wayne was still intact. It had actually intensified, and it really was just the beginning of our work together. I didn't know what it would look like, but this wasn't an end. It was the start of a new chapter and a new adventure.

I cannot begin to tell you how many people have shared with me stories of mystical and spiritual experiences they had since Wayne passed away. In my mind, he became an Ascended

Master, and through his passing he became accessible to even more people than he could reach when he was living. He has visited friends and acquaintances in dreams, been channeled by mediums, and shown up through a multitude of symbols and signs. Some of these signs were anything but subtle—he wanted to make sure people really knew, without a shadow of a doubt, that he was there and available to whoever desired to align with his guidance and love. His loving father and mentor energy is still very much present.

Since the morning that my heart softened, messages from Wayne began to show up in my life, like winks from beyond assuring me of his presence. Especially meaningful is the scent of wild roses in the air when there are no wild roses around. Years ago, Wayne had gifted me with a small vial of rose oil. It is the only physical gift I have from him. He used to carry one with him in his pockets and apply it to his neck and head.

It took months before I stopped crying at the thought of him or when I saw his picture. I didn't understand why it was so difficult—I had only met him a few years prior. Why was it taking so long to grieve him? I had to let go and really allow myself to fully experience the depth of the feelings I had and let them take their course. In some ways it felt silly and inappropriate. Yet, I know many people felt quite similar, wondering why it was so painful to lose someone they barely knew, or in some cases, had never met. It is undeniable he had achieved an incredible depth of intimacy with his readers and listeners. When he passed away, many felt they had lost a close friend.

The deeper I'd go into my meditation and into my heart, the more I could feel Wayne's presence and see how his love from the other side would have an even greater impact on this world. As time went on, I felt the veil getting thinner and thinner, like I was living in a very different reality than before. I had always been supported by guides and higher energies within and around me, but now the evidence of it was tenfold.

It was like Wayne was making sure over and over that I knew he was there for us all in a concrete and clear way.

I'll share with you one more powerful and synchronistic series of events that happened. It was a Sunday morning in winter 2016, and I was in Montreal to speak at a conference at 11:30 A.M. Once again I was nervous and had become ill with a bad cold a few days prior. Just before the conference began, I received a text from my friend Rachel with a picture of a package. She had stumbled upon it in a pile of mail at my old office, now occupied by a massage therapist that she was visiting. I hadn't been in that building for two years. I looked at the picture of the package. It had my name on it, the address of my old office, a Texan sender's address, and a scribbled note at the bottom, "From Wayne." Holy crap! I couldn't believe my eyes. I was so intrigued, but I'd have to wait until I returned to open it.

I was to speak at 11:30 A.M. As I stood on the stage minutes before I was to begin, I felt nervous so I went into my heart and asked, *How may I serve?* I asked for Wayne's guidance with the presentation. Then I opened my eyes and began to speak. I barely remember what I said. It just flowed so effortlessly; I had never experienced such ease onstage before. After the show, when I looked at my e-mails, I saw one from Martin. He said he had a thought of me and Wayne and wanted to let me know. He had sent to me a screenshot of the time: 11:28 A.M.! I hadn't heard from Martin in months, and he did not know I was speaking at this conference. I felt Wayne wanted me to know he'd heard my prayer.

By the end of the day at the conference, I was feeling really drained. But since the program wasn't fully over and I wanted to stay until the end, I excused myself for a minute and headed to the washroom. As I walked up the stairs, I asked Wayne to give me energy to stay for the rest of the day. I wanted to continue to connect with all the people who showed up. As I reached the top of the stairs, I heard, "Anne Berube?" I looked up. "I saw you open for Wayne last year and I have been wanting to offer you a treatment to thank you for bringing him to Montreal ever since. Do you have thirty minutes?" The woman had a reflexology chair all set up, and for the next 30 minutes, I got to rest and replenish. As I lay there, I couldn't believe how immediate the response was!

When I came back down, I found my father, who had been in the audience that day, talking to a woman whom he had randomly met at the event. During their conversation, they realized they had been seated on either side of Wayne at the show last year in Montreal! My father had mentioned there was a woman seated on the other side of Wayne with whom Wayne had shared a bit of his rose oil. I introduced myself, and her name was Rosanne. Of course it was. I shared with them how symbolic and meaningful the rose oil was.

That night on the phone I told Rachel about the magic of the weekend. She said earlier that day she had felt compelled to prepare a vial of rose oil for me and had intended to drop it off with the mysterious package when I returned. She did not know about the rose oil connections. I thought to myself, *This cannot get any stranger.*

When I returned home, Rachel brought the mysterious package over to my house along with the rose oil. She stood in the doorway as I opened it up. There was a book and a letter. I began to read the letter. It was from a man in Texas named Shafeen Ali who had channeled Wayne back in the fall of 2015. This man had written the beautiful book *To Be One with God*, and he was receiving channeled guidance to send the book to a few people. And on that list of names was my name. The letter said, "Please send this letter to my daughter, Anne Berube." I kneeled to the floor. My heart was flooded with love. Other than the small group of people at dinner that night on Maui, no one else knew about the comment he had made!

I called Shafeen on the phone, and he told me that when he heard my name he had to get Wayne to spell it because he had never heard a name like that before. He also knew the name of Wayne's daughters and I wasn't one of them, so he was confused and had to Google me. When he found my name and a picture of me and Wayne, he asked Wayne, "Is this the Anne?" Wayne said yes. Shafeen found my old address on a website and gave it a try.

He wasn't sure the package was going to reach me. I suppose Wayne had made sure it would by guiding Rachel to it. I feel strongly this was a way for Wayne to get my attention because not only were the messages hyperspecific to me and my healing path, but they were relentless. I couldn't ignore his attempt to communicate. That series of events occurred over the span of five days. I felt 100 percent convinced that Wayne was present and active behind the veil. I felt blessed and had tremendous gratitude for his Divine love and his dedication to supporting us.

Wayne had always loved these kinds of things—winks from the universe, messages bringing confirmation of spirit in action here on Earth. It doesn't surprise me he is taking an active role in making them happen now. He's doing it with a sense of style and humor that is unmistakably his own. His gregarious and generous nature is evident in his willingness to show up all over the world, wherever he can be of service.

The biggest lesson I learned from the grieving process is that the language of spirit is love. That spirit communicates through loving feelings, whether it is from loved ones who have passed, guides, Ascended Masters, or the Divine. When I am connected to my heart and in love within my own heart, I become more aware of the guidance available to me.

Wayne, we are blessed by all of your earthly teachings and by your Celestial love. In our hearts you will live forever. I love you.

Thank you, thank you, thank you.

ENDNOTES

———— • ————

Introduction

1. "Soul," *merriam-webster.com*, 2016, accessed December 5, 2016, https://www.merriam-webster.com/dictionary/soul.

Chapter 12

2. English translation: "You see me? Do you see me? I am here. Hug me, hold me in your arms. I want you to be there, I want you. I need you."

Chapter 28

3. Candace B. Pert, *Molecules of Emotion: The Science Behind Mind-Body Medicine*, 1st ed. (New York: Simon & Schuster, 1999), 185.

Chapter 29

4. Candace B. Pert, *Molecules of Emotions: Why You Feel the Way You Feel*, 1st. ed (New York: Scribner, 1997), 187.

Chapter 31

5. Rollin McCraty and Doc Childre, "Coherence: Bridging Personal, Social, and Global Health," *Alternative Therapies* 16, no. 4 (July/August 2010): 15.

Chapter 32

6. Viktor Frankl, *Man's Search for Meaning*, 1st. ed (Boston: Beacon Press, 2006).

7. David Simon, *Free to Love, Free to Heal: Heal Your Body by Healing Your Emotions*, 1st ed. (Carlsbad, CA: Chopra Center Press, 2013).

Chapter 33

8. Take some time to look at the Hubble Telescope website—the imagery that was captured is extraordinary and very telling: www.hubblesite.org.

9. Deepak Chopra, *The Spontaneous Fulfillment of Desire*, 1st ed. (New York: Three Rivers Press, 2003), 191.

10. Ram Dass, *Be Love Now: The Path of the Heart*, 1st ed. (New York: HarperCollins, 2010), 215.

Chapter 37

11. Ramtha, *Ramtha: The White Book* (Yelm, WA: JKZ Publishing, 2005), 187.

Chapter 38

12. Brené Brown, *I Thought It Was Just Me: Women Reclaiming Power and Courage in a Culture of Shame*, 1st Ed. (New York: Gotham Books, 2007), xxiii.

ACKNOWLEDGMENTS

———— • ————

I 'd like to acknowledge the team of people who helped bring this book into the world. My dear friend and very first editor, Renée Hartleib, your love for the writing process and your faith in this book encouraged me to stay the course. Thank you for your unwavering love. Chaz Thorne for your friendship and for helping me find my voice. Reid Tracy for so warmly welcoming me into the Hay House family. Patty Gift for shepherding this book through its publishing process. Lisa Cheng, editor extraordinaire at Hay House, you "got it" from the beginning and you made this editorial adventure so much fun. Thank you for all your hard work. Finally, Anita Moorjani for your loving friendship and your wise teachings. The world is a better place because you shine your light so brightly.

ABOUT THE AUTHOR

———— • ————

Anne Bérubé, Ph.D., is a powerful teacher who has made it her life's purpose to help individuals remember their soul's calling. She has an uncommon ability to share her story and insights in a way that accelerates transformation in others. Through her workshops called the Happy Sessions, she has refined the process of *Be Feel Think Do* and has helped thousands of individuals discover an inner freedom and a connection to their own unique source of wisdom. She lives with her husband and two children in Halifax, Nova Scotia. You can visit her online at anneberube.com.

Hay House Titles of Related Interest

YOU CAN HEAL YOUR LIFE, the movie,
starring Louise Hay & Friends
(available as a 1-DVD program and an expanded 2-DVD set)
Watch the trailer at: www.LouiseHayMovie.com

THE SHIFT, the movie,
starring Dr. Wayne W. Dyer
(available as a 1-DVD program and an expanded 2-DVD set)
Watch the trailer at: www.DyerMovie.com

— • —

WHAT IF THIS IS HEAVEN? How Our Cultural Myths Prevent Us from Experiencing Heaven on Earth, by Anita Moorjani

UNCHARTED: The Journey through Uncertainty to Infinite Possibility, by Colette Baron-Reid

BLOOM: A Tale of Courage, Surrender, and Breaking through Upper Limits, by Bronnie Ware

All of the above are available at your local bookstore or may be ordered by contacting Hay House (see next page).

— • —

We hope you enjoyed this Hay House book. If you'd like to receive our online catalog featuring additional information on Hay House books and products, or if you'd like to find out more about the Hay Foundation, please contact:

Hay House, Inc., P.O. Box 5100, Carlsbad, CA 92018-5100
(760) 431-7695 or (800) 654-5126
(760) 431-6948 (fax) or (800) 650-5115 (fax)
www.hayhouse.com® • www.hayfoundation.org

— • —

Published and distributed in Australia by:
Hay House Australia Pty. Ltd., 18/36 Ralph St., Alexandria NSW 2015
Phone: 612-9669-4299 • *Fax:* 612-9669-4144 • www.hayhouse.com.au

Published and distributed in the United Kingdom by:
Hay House UK, Ltd., Astley House, 33 Notting Hill Gate,
London W11 3JQ • *Phone:* 44-20-3675-2450
Fax: 44-20-3675-2451 • www.hayhouse.co.uk

Published and distributed in the Republic of South Africa by:
Hay House SA (Pty), Ltd., P.O. Box 990, Witkoppen 2068
info@hayhouse.co.za • www.hayhouse.co.za

Published in India by: Hay House Publishers India,
Muskaan Complex, Plot No. 3, B-2, Vasant Kunj, New Delhi 110 070
Phone: 91-11-4176-1620 • *Fax:* 91-11-4176-1630 • www.hayhouse.co.in

Distributed in Canada by:
Raincoast Books, 2440 Viking Way, Richmond, B.C. V6V 1N2
Phone: 1-800-663-5714 • *Fax:* 1-800-565-3770 • www.raincoast.com

— • —

Take Your Soul on a Vacation

Visit www.HealYourLife.com® to regroup, recharge, and reconnect
with your own magnificence. Featuring blogs, mind-body-spirit news,
and life-changing wisdom from Louise Hay and friends.

Visit www.HealYourLife.com today!

9 781401 951153